6/18

D0209833

ALL THE ANSWERS

Michael Kupperman

GALLERY 13
New York   London   Toronto
Sydney   New Delhi

Gallery 13
An Imprint of Simon & Schuster, Inc.
1230 Avenue of the Americas
New York, NY 10020

First Gallery 13 hardcover edition May 2018

GALLERY 13 and colophon are trademarks of Simon & Schuster, Inc.

For information about special discounts for bulk purchases, please contact Simon & Schuster Special Sales at 1-866-506-1949 or business@simonandschuster.com.

The Simon & Schuster Speakers Bureau can bring authors to your live event. For more information or to book an event, contact the Simon & Schuster Speakers Bureau at 1-866-248-3049 or visit our website at www.simonspeakers.com.

Manufactured in the United States of America

1 0 9 8 7 6 5 4 3 2 1

Library of Congress Cataloging-in-Publication Data is available.

ISBN 978-1-5011-6643-3
ISBN 978-1-5011-6644-0 (ebook)

Dedicated to my family
past, present & future

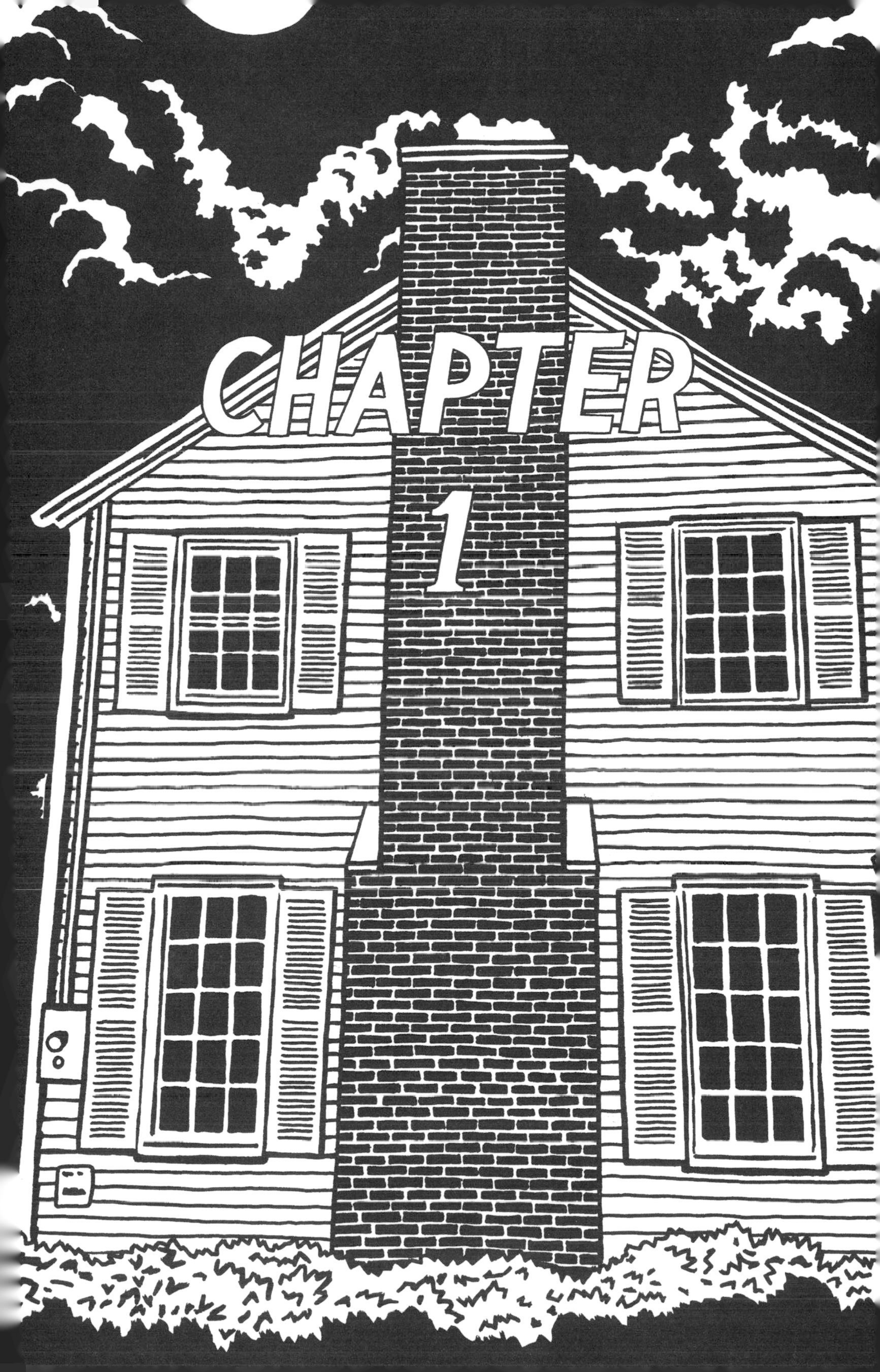
CHAPTER
1

Examinations are formidable even to the best prepared, for the greatest fool may ask more than the wisest man can answer.

—Charles Caleb Colton,
Lacon, 1820

JUNE 2015.
I'M ALONE IN A HOUSE IN THE WOODS.

IT'S THE HOUSE I GREW UP IN.

MY WIFE AND SON HAVE GONE BACK TO THE CITY AND LEFT ME HERE. I HAVE WORK TO DO.

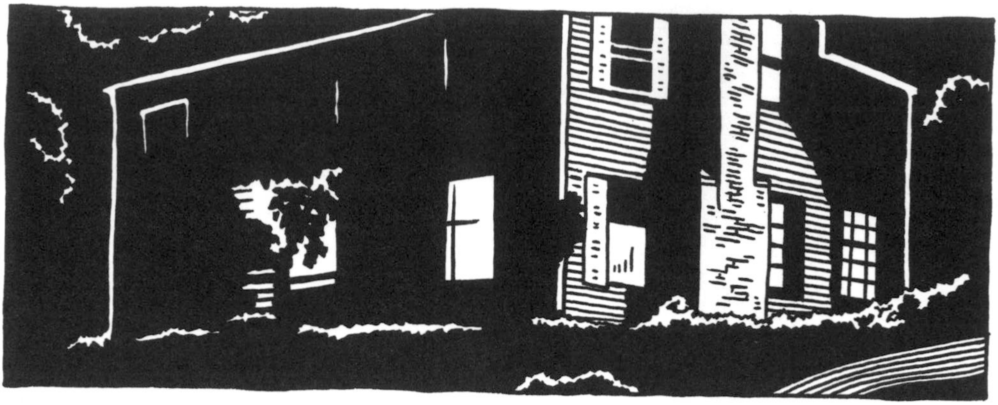

A FEW MILES AWAY IS THE UNIVERSITY OF CONNECTICUT, WHERE MY FATHER TAUGHT FOR FIFTY YEARS.

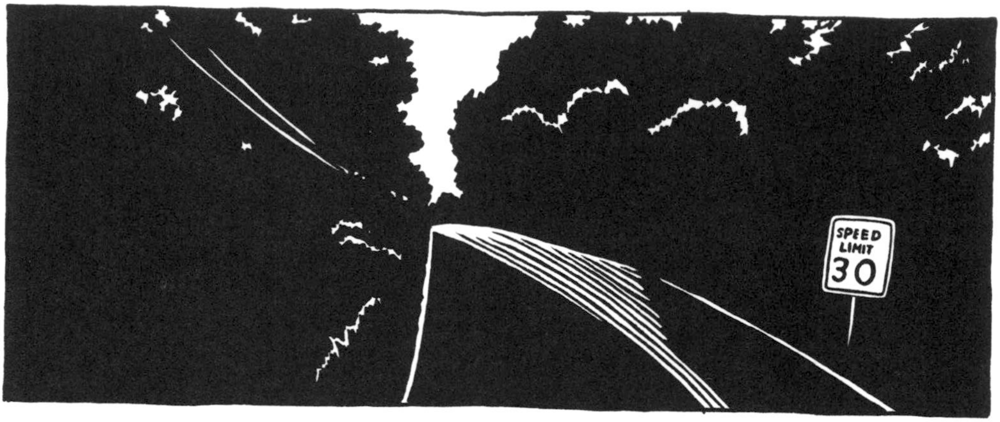
SPEED LIMIT 30

AFTER SO MANY YEARS LIVING IN NEW YORK, I LIKE THE QUIET.

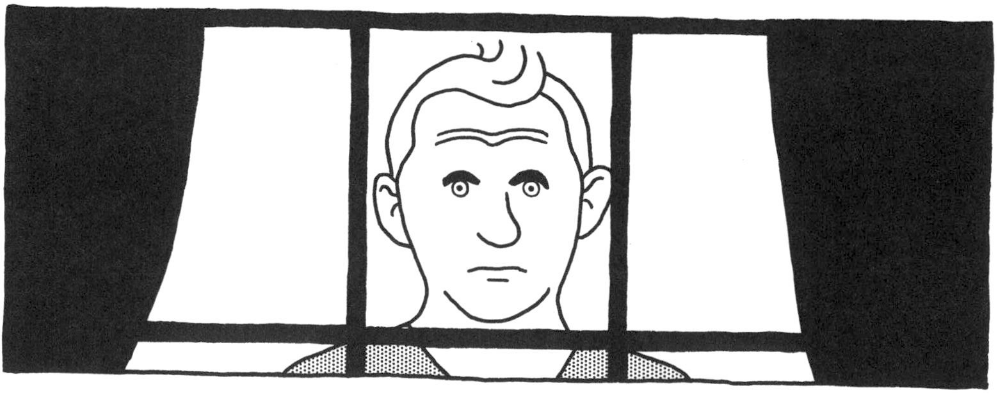

WHEN I WAS A CHILD, IT FELT LIKE WE WERE TRAPPED HERE.

IT FELT LIKE WE WERE HIDING.

MY FATHER HAD THE HOUSE BUILT IN 1964, AND HE WAS THE ONLY ONE WHO SEEMED REALLY AT EASE HERE. HE'D MOST OFTEN BE FOUND SITTING IN THE LIVING ROOM, READING OR LISTENING TO MUSIC.

MY MOTHER WAS ALMOST ALWAYS ANGRY, UNTIL SHE SET HER SIGHTS ON THE CAREER THAT LED THEM AWAY FROM THIS PLACE, TO NEW YORK CITY.

MY WIFE SWEARS THIS HOUSE IS HAUNTED BY THE GHOSTS OF THE UNHAPPY FAMILY WE USED TO BE.

AT ONE CORNER OF THE HOUSE MY FATHER PLACED HIS STUDY. IT'S AN IMPRESSIVE ROOM, WITH BOOKSHELVES COVERING THREE WALLS, FLOOR TO CEILING.

THERE ARE BOOKS ON ART, ARCHITECTURE, SOCIOLOGY, LITERATURE, HISTORY, AND ANTHROPOLOGY.

THERE ARE THE BOOKS HE WROTE DURING HIS CAREER AS A PHILOSOPHER: BOOKS ON CHARACTER, MORALITY, AND ETHICS.

RIGHT NOW I'M PULLING THEM ALL OFF THE SHELVES.

THERE'S SOMETHING HERE I NEED TO FIND. I KNOW THERE IS.

SOMETHING MY FATHER HID AWAY LONG AGO BECAUSE HE COULDN'T DEAL WITH IT.
BECAUSE HE NEEDED TO FORGET.

THERE ARE TWO THINGS I WILL ALWAYS REMEMBER ABOUT THANKSGIVING 2004.
IT WAS JUST ME AND MY PARENTS, MY FATHER AND I SITTING IN AWKWARD SILENCE
WHILE MY MOTHER COOKED.

I TURNED ON THE TV, AND TCM WAS SHOWING
AN ABBOTT AND COSTELLO MOVIE.

MY FATHER SMILED
SLIGHTLY AND SAID:

I COULDN'T BELIEVE MY EARS.

THAT THE LEGENDARY COMEDIANS HAD GIVEN MY FATHER A DOG WASN'T SURPRISING. WHAT WAS WAS THAT MY FATHER HAD JUST MADE A SPONTANEOUS REFERENCE TO EVENTS OF HIS CHILDHOOD WITHOUT ANY APPARENT DISCOMFORT.

HE HAD EVEN SMILED.

THIS HAD NEVER HAPPENED BEFORE.

LATER THAT NIGHT, THE OTHER MEMORABLE THING HAPPENED. I BURST INTO TEARS AT THE DINNER TABLE.

I WAS LONELY AND MISERABLE AND FELT LIKE NOTHING IN MY LIFE HAD WORKED OUT. HERE I WAS, STILL TRAPPED WITH THEM. I WAS A TOTAL LOSER.

I DIDN'T KNOW HOW TO LIVE. I WAS BAD AT IT. WORK WAS STRESS WITHOUT REWARD. I HAD ALMOST NO REAL FRIENDS ANYMORE, EVERYTHING WAS BAD. I WAS DRINKING TOO MUCH.

MY PARENTS DIDN'T KNOW HOW TO REACT, AS USUAL. AFTER A MOMENT I PULLED MYSELF TOGETHER AND WE ALL ACTED AS IF NOTHING HAD HAPPENED.

TWO WEEKS LATER I HELPED MY FRIEND NEIL HANG A SHOW AT CBGB'S GALLERY, AND HIS FRIEND NINA FIXED ME UP WITH HER FRIEND MUIRE.

I WAS LUCKY. VERY, VERY LUCKY.

MY LIFE STARTED TO IMPROVE.

MUIRE AND I MOVED IN TOGETHER. WE GOT MARRIED. WE HAD A CHILD, A BOY.

I WORKED AT BEING BETTER AT LIVING.

MEANWHILE, MY FATHER RETIRED FROM TEACHING. WHEN MY MOTHER WAS HIRED BY NEW YORK UNIVERSITY, HE'D COMMUTED BETWEEN MANSFIELD AND NEW YORK EVERY WEEK. NOW HE WAS IN MANHATTAN MOST OF THE TIME.

I'D NEVER STOPPED THINKING ABOUT WHAT HE'D SAID. HIS CHILDHOOD ADVENTURES HAD BEEN A FORBIDDEN SUBJECT FOR SO MANY YEARS. MAYBE, FINALLY, WE COULD TALK ABOUT IT.

I ASKED HIM IF I COULD INTERVIEW HIM ABOUT *QUIZ KIDS*.

HE SWORE IT DIDN'T BOTHER HIM ANYMORE.   I CHOSE TO BELIEVE HIM.

WE TALKED FOR A WHILE BUT HE HAD VERY LITTLE MEMORY OF ANYTHING. WHEN HE DID REMEMBER PEOPLE, HIS TAKES ON THEM WERE POLITE AND NONCOMMITTAL. HE REFUSED TO PASS JUDGMENT ON ANYONE, BUT HE WAS FRANK AND HONEST... AS MUCH AS HE COULD BE.

IN HIS MIND, HE HAD NOT BEEN A CHILD PRODIGY. HE HAD BEEN GROOMED.

There was no child genius on that show. Certainly not me.

HE SEEMED ALMOST EAGER THAT I DO A BOOK ABOUT IT.

A FEW MONTHS LATER A DOCTOR DIAGNOSED HIM WITH DEMENTIA. I DIDN'T TAKE IT SERIOUSLY AT FIRST. MY FATHER HAD ALWAYS BEEN THE CLASSIC ABSENT-MINDED EGGHEAD. SURELY THIS WAS JUST PART OF THE AGING PROCESS.

ONE AFTERNOON AT THE BROOKLYN BOTANIC GARDEN SHOWED ME HOW WRONG I WAS.

I'M WITH MY PARENTS AND MY SON, AGE FOUR. WE'VE JUST ENTERED THE GARDEN.

MY SON, ALWAYS IN MOTION, RACES UP A SIDE PATH.

EVEN THOUGH HE'LL BE OUT OF SIGHT FOR A MOMENT, WE'RE IN AN ENCLOSED SPACE AND HIS PATH JOINS UP WITH OURS AHEAD, SO I'M NOT WORRIED.

BUT WHEN WE GET TO THE INTERSECTION, HE'S NOWHERE TO BE SEEN.

HE DOESN'T RESPOND WHEN I CALL HIS NAME, OR WHEN I SHOUT IT, OR WHEN I SCREAM IT AS LOUD AS I CAN.

I RUN IN AND OUT OF THE GARDEN, SEARCHING ANYWHERE I THINK HE COULD HAVE GONE.

PART OF ME IS STILL TRAPPED IN THAT MOMENT: RUNNING, SCREAMING, TERRIFIED. I CAN'T LOSE MY BOY.

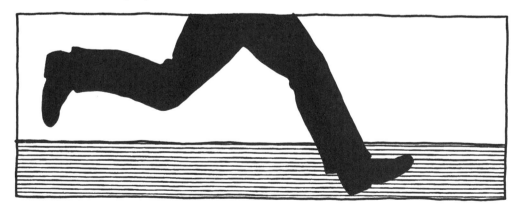

I TELL THE GUARDS, I CALL THE POLICE.

A GUARD OFFERS TO DRIVE ME THROUGH THE GARDEN TO SEE IF I CAN SPOT HIM.

AS WE RIDE THROUGH THE GARDEN IN BRIGHT SUNLIGHT, I CAN'T BREATHE. I'M STARING INTO DARKNESS.

AND THERE HE IS, SMILING AND LAUGHING.

MY BEAUTIFUL SON.

WHAT HAD HAPPENED? WHILE RUNNING ON THE PATH, HE'D SEEN HIS FAVORITE BABYSITTER FAR OFF IN THE DISTANCE, WALKING AWAY...

...AND WITHOUT THINKING, HE'D RUN STRAIGHT TO HER. THEY'D BEEN TOGETHER IN ANOTHER PART OF THE GARDEN. SHE'D BEEN TRYING TO CALL MY WIFE, BUT DIDN'T HAVE MY NUMBER FOR SOME REASON; I DIDN'T CARE. I WAS JUST GRATEFUL MY BOY WAS ALL RIGHT.

WE FIND MY MOTHER, WHO'D BEEN SEARCHING ON HER OWN, AND GO BACK TO WHERE I'D LEFT MY FATHER WAITING FOR THE POLICE.

BUT HE'S GONE, AND HIS PHONE IS SWITCHED OFF.

NOW I SEE HOW THINGS ARE. HOW THEY'RE GOING TO BE FROM NOW ON.

I REPEAT EVERYTHING I'D DONE BEFORE FOR MY SON, SEARCHING EVERYWHERE. I CALL HIS PHONE AGAIN AND AGAIN.

NINETY MINUTES LATER HE FINALLY ANSWERS, AND STARTS DIALING.

IT TURNS OUT HE HAD JUST GOTTEN ON THE SUBWAY AND GONE HOME.

MINGLING WITH MY EXHAUSTION AND TENSION WAS A FAMILIAR FEELING: DISAPPOINTMENT.

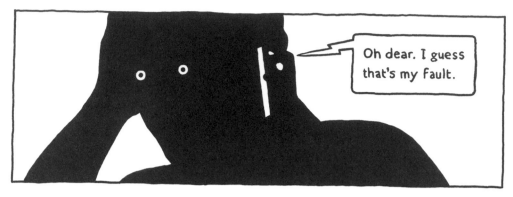

I'D HOPED MY FATHER WAS LETTING HIS WALLS DOWN, THAT MAYBE WE'D FINALLY START TO BECOME CLOSER.

NOW HE WAS SKIPPING INTO BLISSFUL AMNESIA, WHILE I STILL HAD SO MANY UNANSWERED QUESTIONS AND UNRESOLVED FEELINGS.

WHY DID I FEEL LIKE THIS ALL HAD TO DO WITH HIS CHILDHOOD AND *QUIZ KIDS*?

I BEGAN RESEARCHING. MAYBE IF I ASKED THE RIGHT QUESTIONS, HIT THE RIGHT TRIGGERS, I COULD SPARK SOMETHING INSIDE HIM.

TWO YEARS LATER, HERE I AM, STILL LOOKING FOR ANSWERS.

THE SHELVES IN MY FATHER'S STUDY INTERSECT IN A WAY THAT PROVIDES PLENTY OF HIDING SPACE. I'VE SEARCHED EVERY OTHER INCH OF THE HOUSE; ANYTHING HE'S BURIED IS IN HERE.

SO FAR I'VE FOUND:

A NAZI BADGE. MANY SOLDIERS WHO'D LISTENED TO HIM ON THE RADIO OVERSEAS SENT HIM BATTLEFIELD MEMENTOS WHEN THEY RETURNED.

A SHOEBOX WITH SOME JUNK AND THE KEYS TO TWO CITIES.

A FEW SEVENTY-YEAR-OLD SIGNED BASEBALLS.

A XEROX OF *BECOMING HUMAN*, THE AUTOBIOGRAPHY MY FATHER TRIED TO WRITE IN 1974. IN IT HE CALLS *QUIZ KIDS* "THE MOST FORMIDABLE LIMITING FACTOR IN MY LIFE."

THE LANGUAGE HE USES SEEMS DESIGNED TO HOLD BACK ANY FEELINGS AROUSED IN HIM BY THE SUBJECT MATTER.

AFTER TWO SHORT CHAPTERS HE GIVES UP, THE IMMENSITY OF EXPRESSING WHAT HE HAD BEEN THROUGH CLEARLY TOO MUCH FOR HIM.

BUT THE BIGGEST DISCOVERY IS IN THE VERY LAST PLACE I LOOK: THE UPPER-LEFT CORNER OF THE SHELVES. I MOVE SOME ART BOOKS AND THERE THEY ARE...

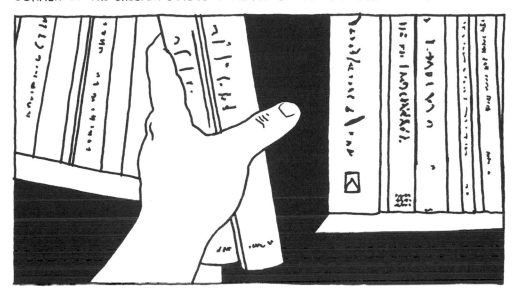

FIVE MASSIVE, CRUMBLING SCRAPBOOKS. FLAKES DRIFT OFF AS I PULL THEM FROM THEIR HIDING PLACE.

THE HEIGHT OF MY FATHER'S FAME WAS WHEN AMERICANS WERE BEING TOLD TO RECYCLE ALL PAPER FOR THE WAR EFFORT. ONLY ONE PERSON WOULD'VE SAVED ALL THIS STUFF.

THE ONE WHO MASTERMINDED IT ALL.

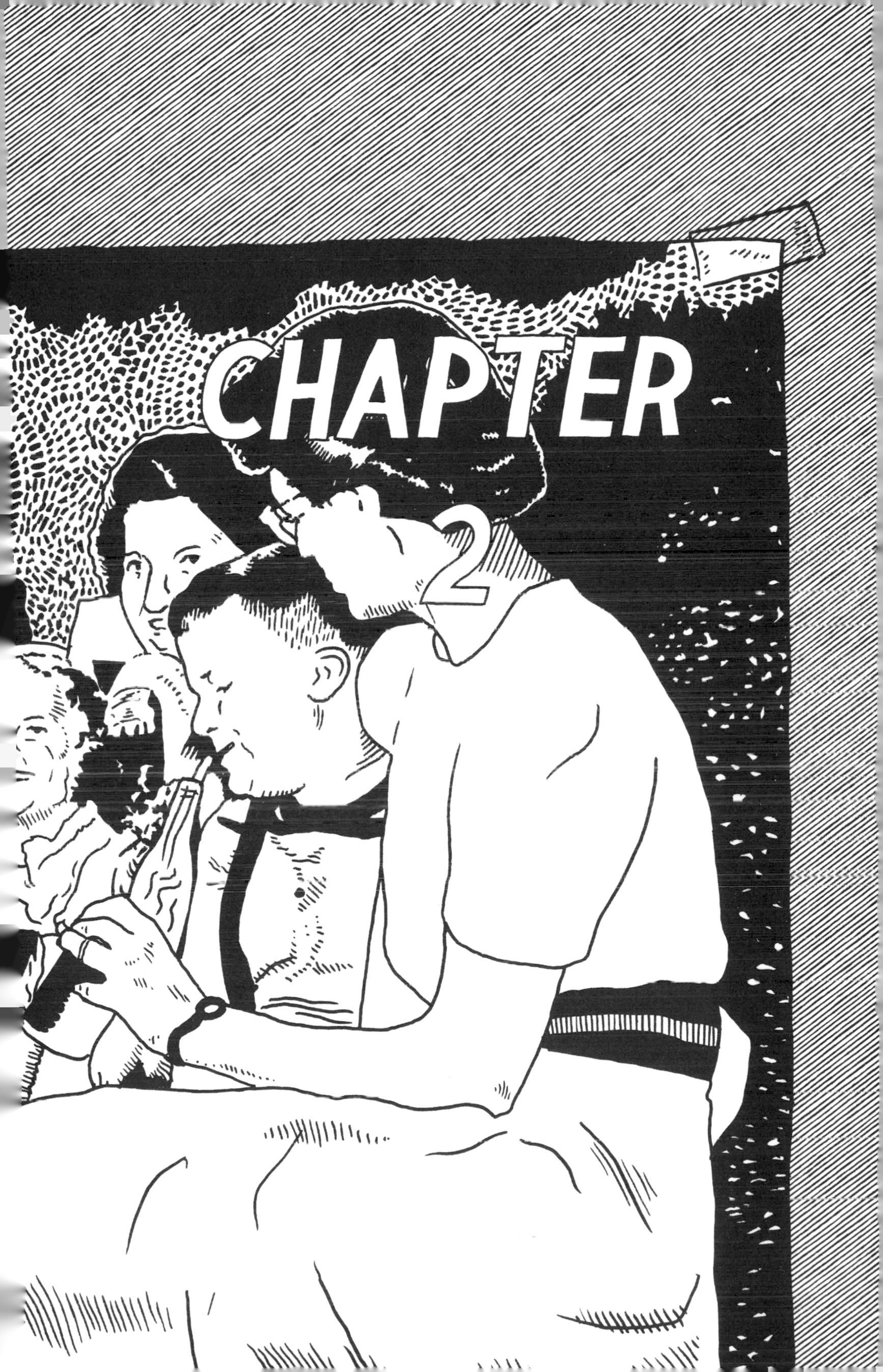
CHAPTER
2

The Matron of Honor spoke up from the other side of the room, from the invisible, dusty recesses of the couch. "I'd like to see a kid of *mine* get on one of those crazy programs," she said. "Or *act*. Any of those things. I'd die, in fact, before I'd let any child of mine turn themself into a little exhibitionist before the public. It warps their whole entire lives."

—J. D. Salinger,
Raise High the Roof Beam, Carpenters

IT'S ALL HERE.

EVERY NEWSPAPER STORY, MAGAZINE ARTICLE, PRESS RELEASE. EVERY TICKET, SCHEDULE, SCRIPT.

EVERY LETTER, NOTE, TELEGRAM. EVERY PIECE OF PAPER, EVERY PHOTOGRAPH.

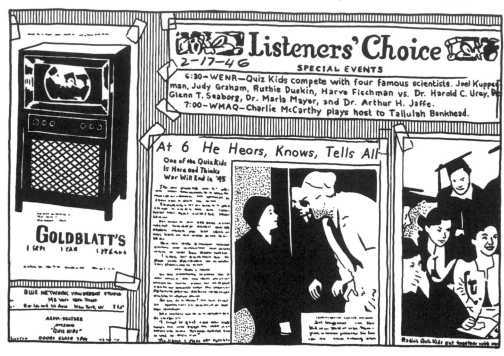

IT'S OVERWHELMING.

SO MANY PICTURES OF MY DAD. WEIRD, STAGED PUBLICITY PHOTOS, SOME IN QUESTIONABLE TASTE.

PICTURES OF HIM WITH ACTORS, SINGERS, COMEDIANS, SOLDIERS, REPORTERS, POLITICIANS...

PICTURES OF HIM WITH THE OTHER QUIZ KIDS, DOING THE SHOW AND ON TOUR.

PICTURES OF MY GRANDPARENTS, MORE THAN I'VE EVER SEEN.

PICTURES OF THE GRANDFATHER I NEVER KNEW...

...AND THE GRANDMOTHER I BARELY DID.

EVEN AS A YOUNG CHILD, I COULD SEE THAT GRANDMA SARA WAS A PERSON WHO RADIATED TENSION.

SHE WAS THE ONE PERSON IN THE FAMILY STILL TALKING ABOUT *QUIZ KIDS*, EVEN THOUGH IT MADE MY DAD VERY UNCOMFORTABLE.

I UNDERSTOOD THAT SHE HAD SABOTAGED EVERY ROMANCE HE'D HAD; THIS WAS WHY SHE HADN'T MET MY SHIKSA MOTHER UNTIL THE DAY OF THEIR WEDDING.

I FELT NO CONNECTION TO MY GRANDMOTHER, BECAUSE IT SEEMED CLEAR I WASN'T SUPPOSED TO.

SHE WAS THE ONE WHO'D BEEN FILLING THESE SCRAPBOOKS. OBSESSIVELY CHRONICLING EVERY DETAIL OF THE CAREER SHE'D PLANNED.

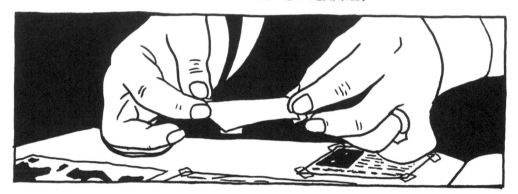

THE DAUGHTER OF IMMIGRANTS, SHE'D WANTED TO BE A DANCER, BUT HAD GIVEN IT UP TO HELP RAISE HER SIBLINGS WHEN THEIR FATHER WALKED OUT ON THEM DURING THE DEPRESSION. LATER SHE PUT THAT ENERGY INTO BEING A TIRELESS STAGE MOTHER.

THE PHRASE "CHILD PRODIGY" FIRST APPEARED IN THE 1860S, ATTACHED TO THE IMMIGRANT PREPUBESCENT PERFORMERS FEATURED ON URBAN MUSIC HALL STAGES.

BY THE 1920S, THERE WERE "CHILD PRODIGIES" EVERYWHERE. PRODIGIES IN SPORTS, SCIENCE, THE ARTS, MATH...FOR AN IMMIGRANT FAMILY, A PRODIGY WAS AN OPPORTUNITY FOR ADVANCEMENT, LIKE FINDING A GOLDEN TICKET.

THE MYTHOLOGY OF MY FATHER'S DEVELOPMENT, TOLD AND RETOLD IN THE YEARS FOLLOWING HIS DISCOVERY, FIT THE IDEALS OF THE AGE PERFECTLY. MY GRANDFATHER, A CIVIL ENGINEER, STARTED TEACHING HIM MATH AT NIGHT. FROM THEN ON, HIS GIFT FLOWERED WITHOUT ASSISTANCE, A SERIES OF SURPRISES—ALMOST LIKE MIRACLES.

HE'D BEEN OVERHEARD LULLING HIMSELF TO SLEEP BY SINGING MULTIPLICATION TABLES.

HE CAUGHT THE GROCER CHEATING HIS MOTHER WHEN HE WAS FOUR.

HE DISCOVERED ERRORS IN A MATH TEXTBOOK.

FINALLY, HIS KINDERGARDEN TEACHER SUGGESTED HE WRITE TO *QUIZ KIDS*. HE WAS FIVE.

QUIZ KIDS WAS A RADIO PROGRAM BROADCAST OUT OF CHICAGO, WHERE THEY LIVED. MY FATHER'S FIRST APPEARANCE ON IT WAS APRIL 29, 1942.

THE SHOW INVOLVED QUESTIONS IN OTHER SUBJECTS BESIDES MATH, SO HE DIDN'T SCORE HIGH ENOUGH TO COME BACK; BUT THE PRODUCERS GAVE HIS MOTHER A LIST OF BOOKS TO READ, TOLD HER WHAT TO DO TO PREPARE HIM TO RETURN.

WHEN HE CAME BACK, HE SCORED HIGH IN ALL SUBJECTS AND QUICKLY BECAME A REGULAR.

QUIZ KIDS HAD BEEN ON SINCE AUGUST 1940. THE FORMAT WAS SIMPLE: FIVE KIDS COMPETED TO ANSWER QUESTIONS SENT IN BY LISTENERS. THE TOP THREE CAME BACK FOR THE NEXT SHOW.

NOBODY WON ANYTHING; THERE WERE NO PRIZES BEYOND BEING ALLOWED TO COME BACK. EVERY PARTICIPANT RECEIVED A $100 WAR BOND (WORTH $75). THE QUIZMASTER WAS GENIAL JOE KELLY, A PERFORMER SINCE AGE SIX. HIS JOLLY, GEE-SHUCKS DELIVERY HELPED MAKE THE SHOW A HIT.

THE CHIEF QUIZZER

IT WENT LIKE THIS:

FIRST A BELL RINGING, THEN AN ORGAN PLAYING "SCHOOL DAYS."

We're on the air with the school kids questionnaire! Brought to you by the makers of Alka-Seltzer and One-a-Day vitamins!

And here they are—the Quiz Kids!

GERARD AGE 10 · JOEL AGE 6 · TOMMY AGE 10 · CLAUDE AGE 14

Now the classroom's in charge of our chief quizzer himself... Joe Kelly!

Thank you, Fort Pearson, and good evening, everyone!

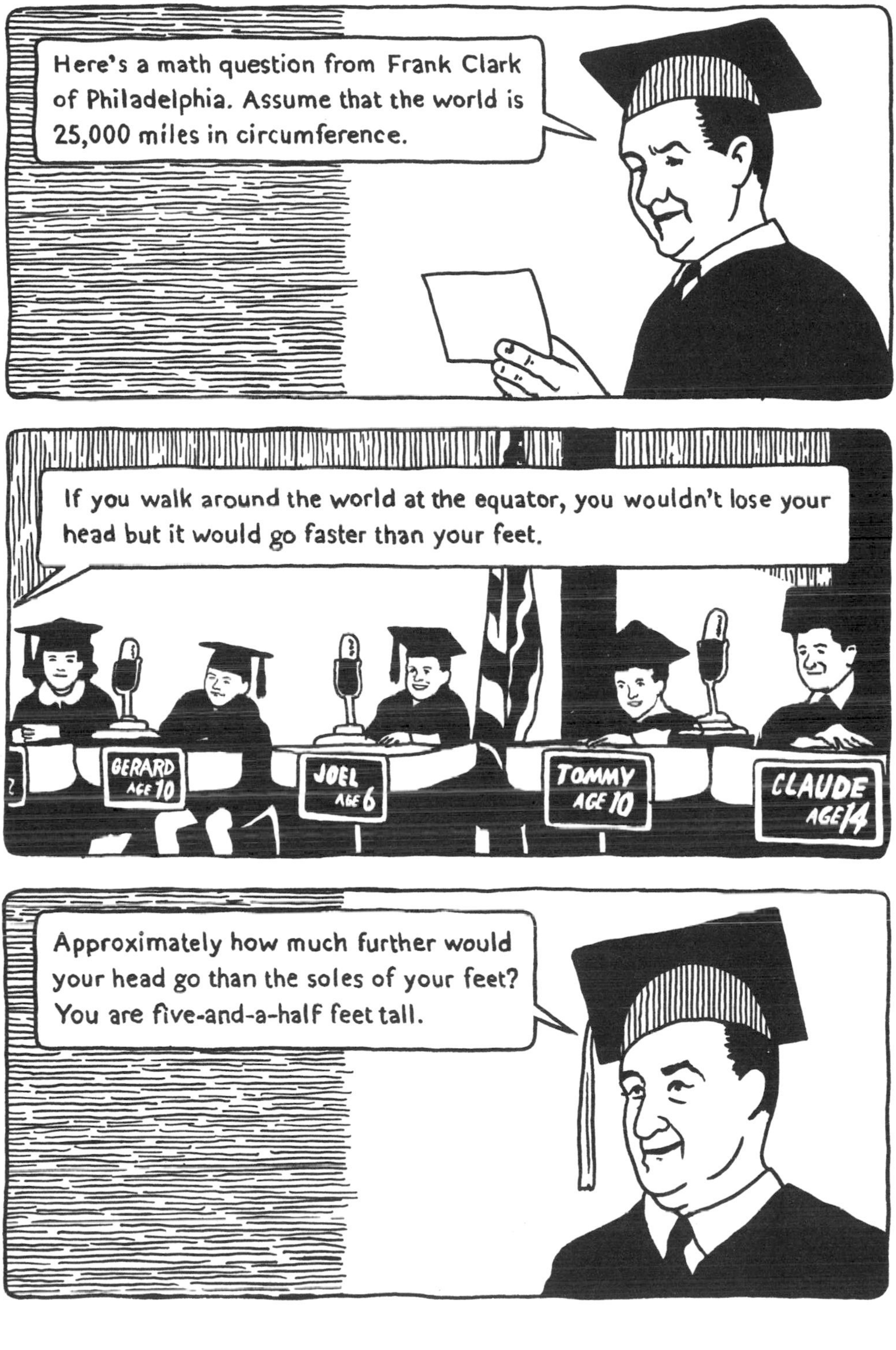
Here's a math question from Frank Clark of Philadelphia. Assume that the world is 25,000 miles in circumference.
If you walk around the world at the equator, you wouldn't lose your head but it would go faster than your feet.
GERARD AGE 10
JOEL AGE 6
TOMMY AGE 10
CLAUDE AGE 14
Approximately how much further would your head go than the soles of your feet? You are five-and-a-half feet tall.

A STAR WAS BORN.

THE PRESS WENT CRAZY FOR HIM. THEY RHAPSODIZED ABOUT HIS INTELLIGENCE. THEY COMPARED HIM TO THE GREATEST MINDS IN HISTORY.

THEY CAME UP WITH INANE NICKNAMES FOR HIM: BABY EINSTEIN. MIDGET EUCLID. MATHEMAGICIAN. THE HUMAN COMPTOMETER. BY 1943, HE WAS RECEIVING 10,000 PIECES OF FAN MAIL A WEEK.

IF MY GRANDPARENTS HAD SET OUT TO CREATE A CHILD PRODIGY, THEY HAD SUCCEEDED BEYOND THEIR WILDEST DREAMS. HE WAS SOON THE MOST FAMOUS PRODIGY IN AMERICA, AND POSSIBLY THE WORLD.

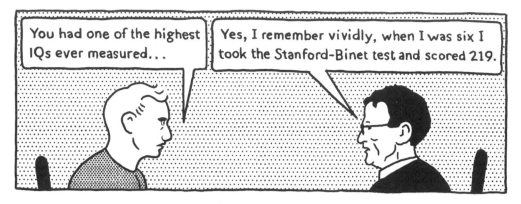

You had one of the highest IQs ever measured...

Yes, I remember vividly, when I was six I took the Stanford-Binet test and scored 219.

But later I took a test on objects in space, spatial judgments, and I was below average. I was good with words and numbers but not that.

There's this weird notion that intelligence is a single thing, but in fact people can be smart in some ways and stupid in others.

What did I know... obviously as much as a kid my age could know, plus a lot of facts... I had a good memory for all sorts of crap.

I was told to read *Time* magazine regularly, and I did it.

ONLY ONE OTHER QUIZ KID HAD RECEIVED THE KIND OF BUILDUP MY FATHER HAD:
GERARD DARROW, CHILD SPECIALIST IN WILDLIFE AND ORNITHOLOGY.

GERARD WAS AN ECCENTRIC BOY WITH NO MOTHER, WHO LIVED WITH HIS FATHER
AND A COLLECTION OF RELATIVES. AT FIRST EVERYONE LOVED HIM TOO.

BUT HIS STAR FELL AS MY FATHER'S ROSE. IT DIDN'T HELP THAT GERARD HAD BECOME
SMUG AND CONCEITED, OR THAT HE DESPISED REPORTERS AND LOVED MESSING WITH
THEM.

GERARD'S AUNT SAW MY FATHER AS GETTING PREFERENTIAL TREATMENT, RESULTING IN BACKSTAGE DRAMA. IT DIDN'T HELP. SOON GERARD WAS FIRED. HE WAS ELEVEN, FIVE YEARS SHORT OF THE OFFICIAL "GRADUATION AGE" FOR QUIZ KIDS.

THIRTY YEARS LATER HE TALKED TO STUDS TERKEL FOR HIS ORAL HISTORY, *WORKING.* HE WAS STILL VERY BITTER.

I was exploited. I can't forgive those who exploited me.

HIS LIFE HAD NOT GONE WELL. HE'D BEEN UNABLE TO HOLD ON TO JOBS OR RELATIONSHIPS. LONELY AND DRINKING HEAVILY, HE DIED SOON AFTER.

Reporters poking and prodding you...as a child you can't cope with these things.

MY FATHER WAS NEVER THE KIND TO FEEL SORRY FOR HIMSELF. BUT I NOW KNOW HE FEELS HE WAS EXPLOITED TOO. WHEN WE HAD TALKED ABOUT *QUIZ KIDS*, HE HAD A THEORY FOR WHY HIS STARDOM HAD HAPPENED.

ONCE HE'D SPOKEN THOSE WORDS ALOUD, IT WAS LIKE A DOOR HAD BEEN OPENED. HE REPEATED THEM EVERY TIME I SAW HIM OVER THE NEXT FEW MONTHS.

THIS WAS BEFORE I'D DONE ANY RESEARCH...

BEFORE I'D STARTED TRYING TO DECIPHER HISTORY.

CHAPTER 3

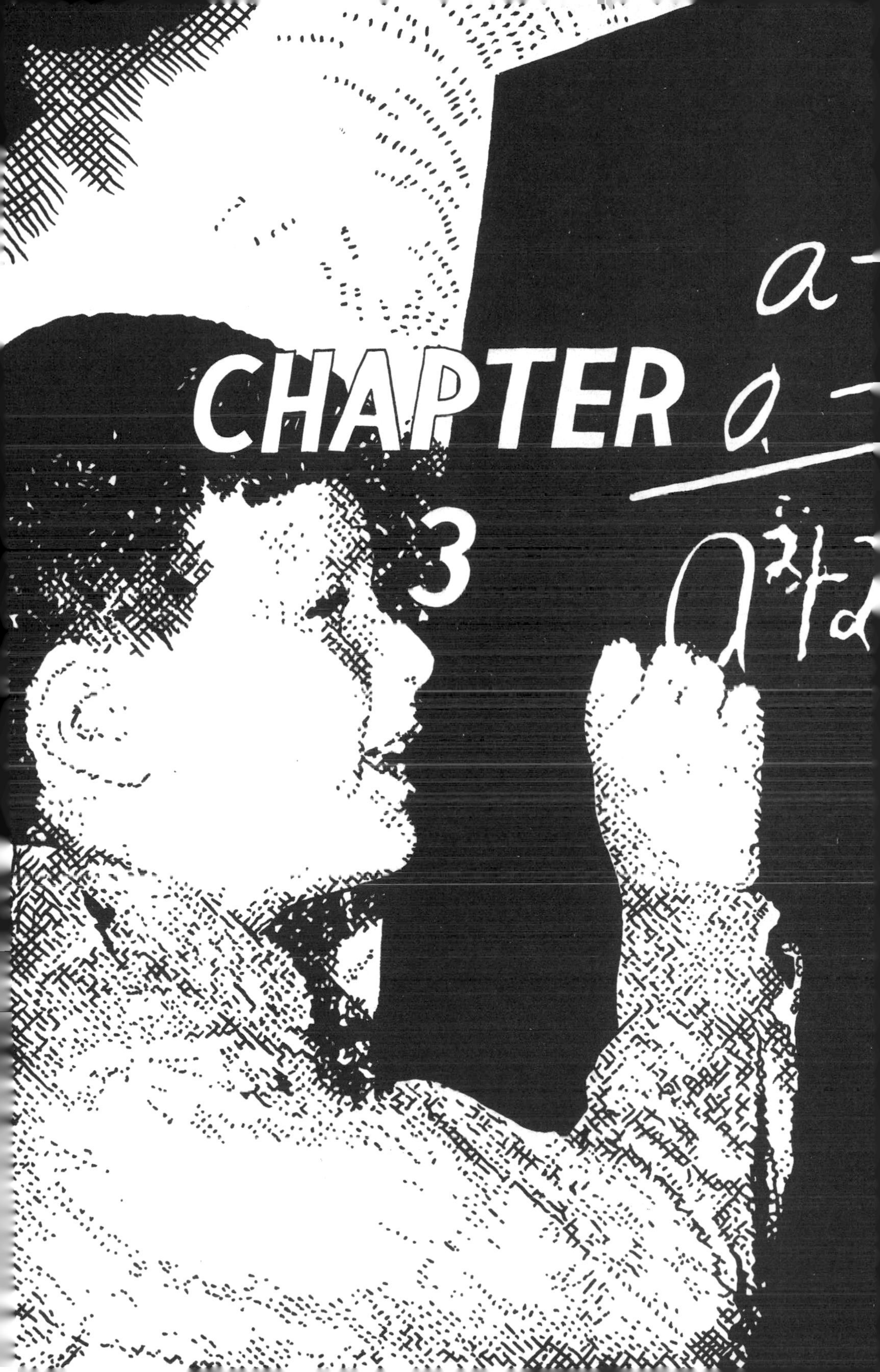

These young people are new people sent to this scene by Destiny to take our places. They come with new visions to fulfill, new powers to exploit.

—Henry Ford, 1924

AMERICA IN THE FIRST FEW DECADES OF THE TWENTIETH CENTURY WAS A COUNTRY STILL STRUGGLING WITH ITS FEELINGS TOWARD JEWS.

THIS WAS AT LEAST PARTLY DUE TO CAR MANUFACTURER HENRY FORD, WHO'D DONE HIS BEST TO PROVOKE HATRED WITH A PRODIGIOUS FLOOD OF ANTI-SEMITIC LITERATURE IN THE 1920s, DISTRIBUTED THROUGH FORD DEALERSHIPS.

FORD HATED JEWS. TO HIM THEY WERE A SINISTER FORCE THAT NEEDED TO BE EXPOSED. THEY IMPEDED THE FLOW OF BUSINESS.

HIS IDEAS TRAVELED AROUND THE WORLD, AND HELPED INSPIRE THE HORROR THAT DEVELOPED IN EUROPE.

THE WORDS MY FATHER HAD BEEN SAYING TOOK A WHILE TO SETTLE IN MY BRAIN.

THAT SEEMED TO ME LIKE WHAT ANY EX-CHILD PERFORMER WOULD SAY. THEN I STARTED READING ABOUT *QUIZ KIDS* PRODUCER **LOUIS G. COWAN.**

AND WHAT MY FATHER HAD BEEN SAYING SUDDENLY MADE A LOT MORE SENSE.

COWAN—BORN COHEN—ALMOST CERTAINLY THE SMARTEST PERSON IN THIS BOOK, WAS THE CAUSE OF NEARLY EVERYTHING THAT HAPPENS IN IT.

QUIZ KIDS HAD BEEN HIS IDEA. HE WAS ALWAYS INVENTING NEW FORMATS.

HE SAW THE WAR AS A STRUGGLE OF SURVIVAL FOR THE JEWISH RACE.

DURING THE WAR, COWAN WAS ONE OF THE PEOPLE IN CHARGE OF RADIO PROPAGANDA, BOTH ABROAD AND AT HOME.

HE PRODUCED BIG, FUN SHOWS TO ENTERTAIN THE TROOPS...

...AND INCLUDED PLENTY OF MISINFORMATION FOR ENEMY EARS.

AT HOME HE PUSHED POSITIVE IMAGES OF SERVICEMEN, MINORITIES, THE WAR EFFORT.

SO WAS MY FATHER PROPAGANDA? I NOW THINK HE WAS.

WHETHER BY DESIGN OR ACCIDENT, HE WAS A SYMBOL BECAUSE OF HIS RACE.

WHY ELSE WOULD A FAIRLY CUTE KID WITH IMPRESSIVE MATH SKILLS BECOME SUCH A NATIONAL OBSESSION? NOT JUST GOOFING OFF ON THE RADIO, BUT MEETING IMPORTANT MEN WHO RAN THE COUNTRY.

ONLY IF HE'S JEWISH, AND IT'S WORLD WAR II.

THERE WAS A SENTIMENTALITY ATTACHED TO HIM BECAUSE OF THE WAR AND HIS ETHNICITY. IT DEFINED HIM.

I'M SURE HE WAS TOLD REPEATEDLY:

You being on that show is good for the Jews!

IT'S HARD FOR PEOPLE TO BE AS INDIFFERENT TO KIDS AS THEY ARE TO ADULTS.

JEWISH JOURNALISTS MADE SURE TO FEATURE HIM WHENEVER POSSIBLE. THEY TOOK CUTE THINGS OTHER QUIZ KIDS HAD SAID AND PUT THEM IN MY FATHER'S MOUTH.

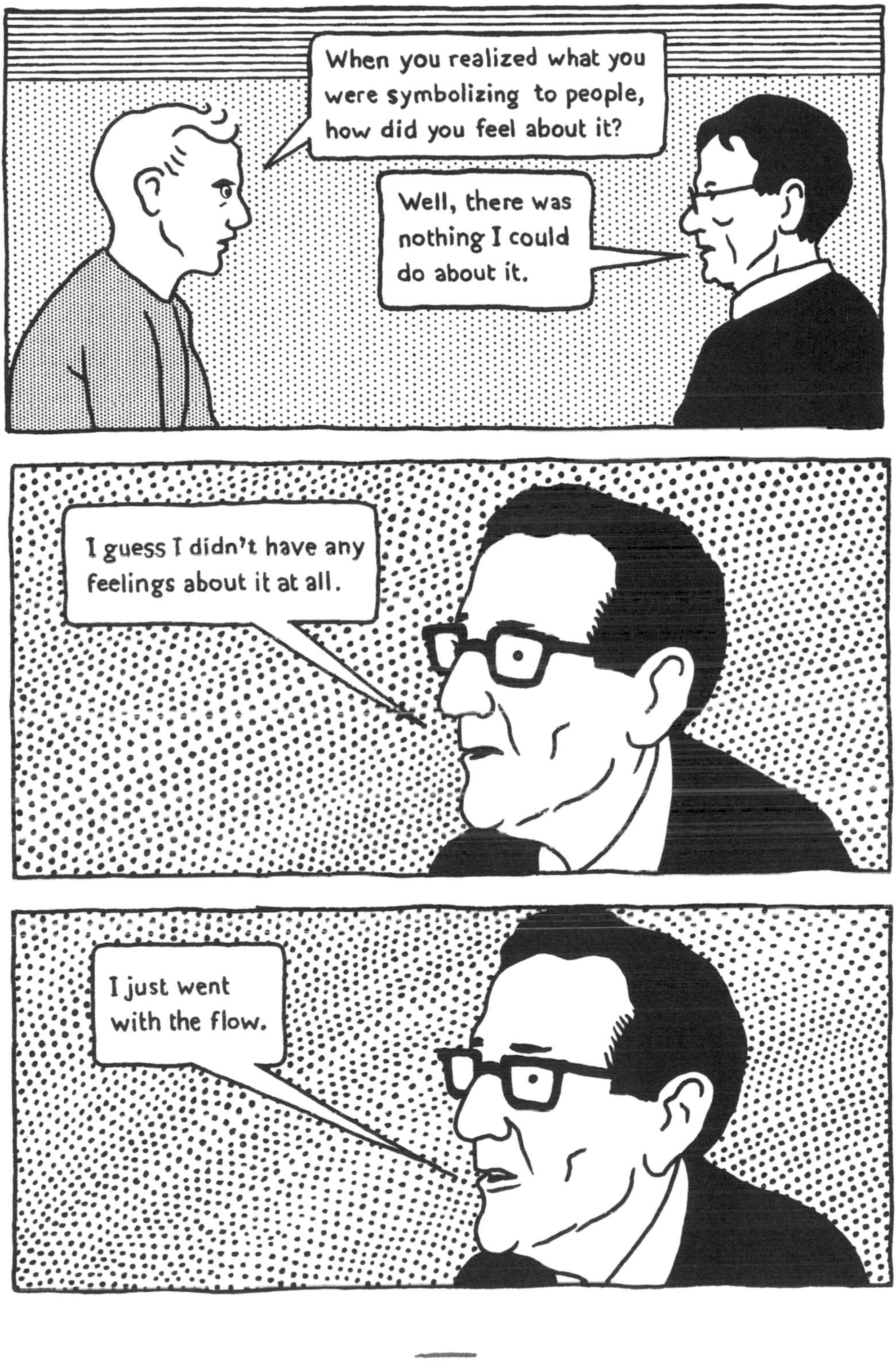
When you realized what you were symbolizing to people, how did you feel about it?
Well, there was nothing I could do about it.
I guess I didn't have any feelings about it at all.
I just went with the flow.

CERTAINLY *QUIZ KIDS* WAS UNDISGUISED PROPAGANDA FOR THE WAR, AND FOR THE PLIGHT OF EUROPE'S JEWS.

...it was five days before Hitler came over, that was the last time I saw my grandmother.

GERARD AGE 10

SMYLLA AGE 15

JC

THE MAIN KIDS—RUTHIE DUSKIN, HARVE FISCHMAN, RICHARD WILLIAMS, AND MY DAD—TOURED THE COUNTRY SELLING WAR BONDS.

THEY VISITED HOSPITALS, SHIPYARDS, FACTORIES, MILITARY AND NAVAL BASES.

THEY VISITED THE SENATE AND THE WHITE HOUSE.

RICHARD WAS THE ONLY ONE WHO WASN'T JEWISH. IT WASN'T UNCOMMON TO HEAR SOMEONE IN THE CROWD SHOUT:

MAYBE PEOPLE NEEDED TO SEE AND HEAR JEWS, TO KNOW THAT THEY WERE ACTUAL HUMAN BEINGS.

PUTTING CHILDREN ON DISPLAY FOR THE INTEREST AND AMUSEMENT OF ADULTS WAS MORE COMMONPLACE BACK THEN. IN CANADA, FOLLOWING THE BIRTH OF FIVE SURVIVING QUINTUPLETS (A FIRST), THE GOVERNMENT PUT THEM ON DISPLAY BEHIND GLASS FOR THOUSANDS OF DAILY VISITORS TO GAWK AT.

"QUINTLAND" CLOSED IN 1943, WHEN THE QUINTS WERE EIGHT.

WHEN THE QUIZ KIDS APPEARED IN DETROIT IN 1943, THEY WERE INVITED TO TOUR THE B-24 PLANT IN DEARBORN AND MEET HENRY FORD, WHO HAD AN OFFICE THERE.

FORD HAD BEEN TRYING TO REPAIR HIS IMAGE BY REVERSING HIS STANCE ON JEWS. "THERE IS A NEED FOR THE JEW IN THIS WORLD" HE HAD ANNOUNCED IN 1941.

STILL, THE QUIZ KIDS WERE NERVOUS. AS THEY ENTERED FORD'S OFFICE, THEY CLUSTERED BEHIND RICHARD, THE GENTILE, FOR SAFETY. BUT FORD WAS FRIENDLY.

How do you do, Quiz Kids! I like to meet people who live such busy and useful lives!

You're one to say that, when that's the kind of life you've always lived!

Where's Joel Kupperman?

He had a bad cold, and his mother wouldn't let him come. He's terribly disappointed.

Well so am I!

We're going to tell him everything about you and Willow Run...

THE NEXT MORNING FORD SHOWED UP AT MY DAD'S HOTEL.

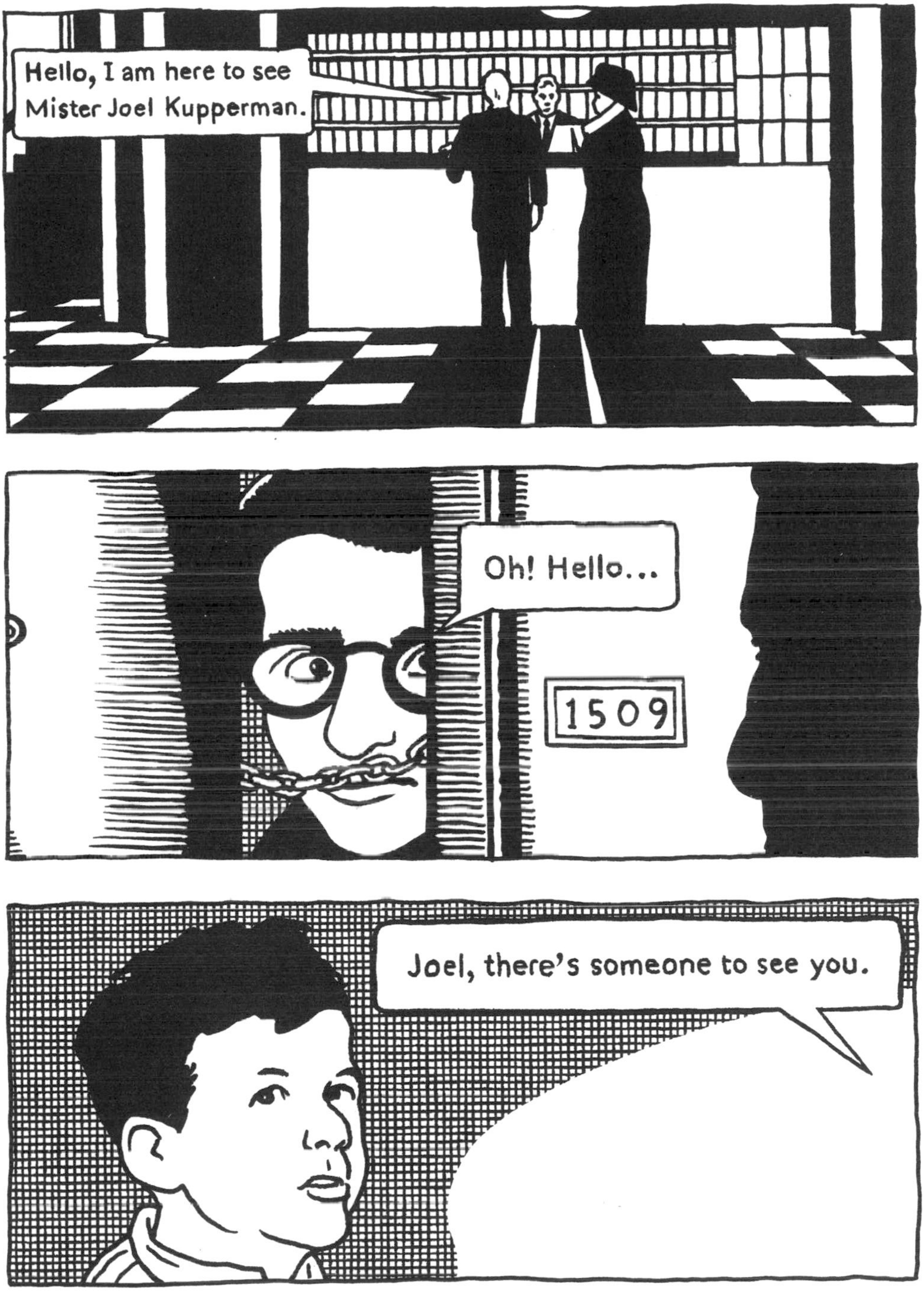
Hello, I am here to see Mister Joel Kupperman.
Oh! Hello...
1509
Joel, there's someone to see you.

WHAT DID THEY TALK ABOUT, THE ANTI-SEMITIC INDUSTRIALIST AND THE JEWISH CHILD PRODIGY? WHAT DID THEY THINK OF EACH OTHER?

THERE'S NO WAY OF KNOWING. MY GRANDMOTHER NEVER RECORDED HER IMPRESSIONS OF ANYTHING. SHE ONLY COLLECTED OTHER PEOPLE'S.

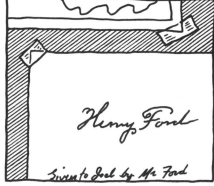

AND ANY IMPRESSIONS MY FATHER HAD FORMED WERE ERASED A LONG TIME AGO.

HE'S NEVER BEEN COMFORTABLE WITH UNPLEASANT THOUGHTS.

IF A PERSON OR SITUATION MAKES HIM FEEL BAD, HE'LL REMOVE HIMSELF FROM IT.

THE QUIZ KIDS DIDN'T SEEM TROUBLED BY ALL THE ATTENTION. THEY SEEMED TO BE GOOD FRIENDS HAVING AMAZING ADVENTURES TOGETHER.

AFTER IT WAS ALL OVER, MY DAD NEVER TALKED TO ANY OF THEM AGAIN.

THERE WERE MEET-UPS. THERE WERE REUNIONS.

HE AVOIDED THEM ALL.

HE LEFT HIS JEWISHNESS BEHIND TOO. IT WAS SOMETHING ELSE THAT WAS NEVER DISCUSSED IN OUR HOUSE.

I HAVE NO IDEA WHAT IT MEANS TO BE JEWISH. I FEEL NO CONNECTION WITH THAT SIDE OF MY HERITAGE.

UNTIL I DID THIS RESEARCH, I HAD NO IDEA HE'D BEEN A HUGE BASEBALL FAN, AND EVEN PLAYED PIANO WITH REASONABLE SKILL. THIS WAS ALL NEWS TO ME.

HE ERASED EVERYTHING, BUT THAT LEFT HIM WITH NOTHING TO SHARE WITH ME.

A MEMORY FROM THE EARLY '70S.

NOW HE'S LOSING HIS MIND TO ESCAPE ME UNDERSTANDING HIM.

WELL FUCK THAT. I WILL UNDERSTAND ME.

DID I SAY ME? I MEANT HIM.

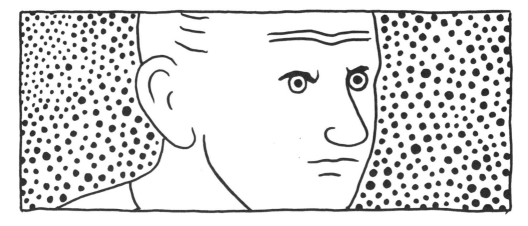

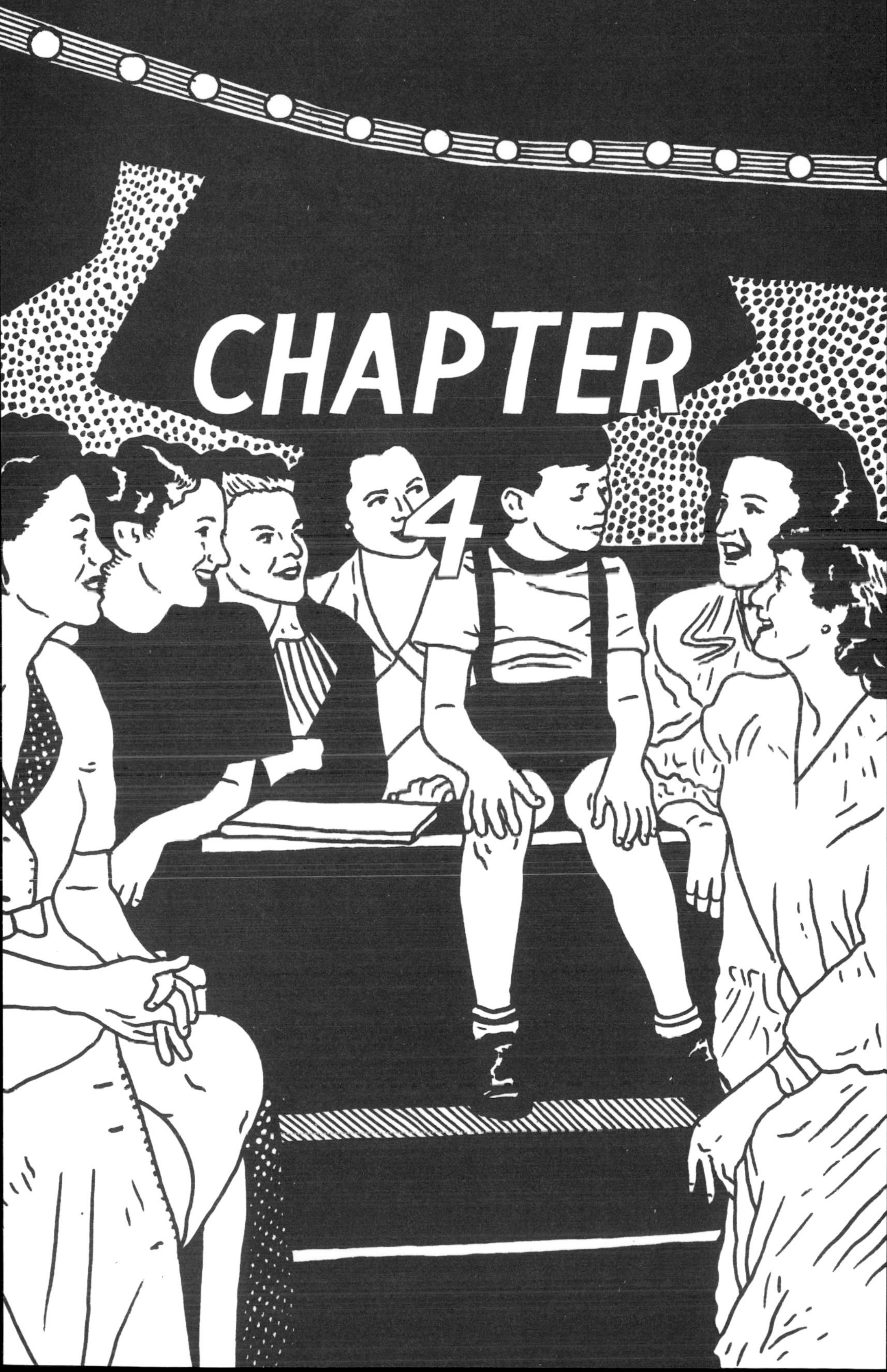
CHAPTER
4

"Zuck. Zuck—it just now dawned on me. I'm sorry. I'm in a terrible state of confusion. Joel Kupperman—remember? I used to call you Joel Kupperman, the Quiz Kid."

"That's right."

"Sure, you had all the answers."

—Philip Roth, *The Anatomy Lesson*

ITEMS continued

THE IDEA I'D HAD—THAT MY FATHER NO LONGER CARED ABOUT HIS CHILDHOOD—
HAD OBVIOUSLY BEEN UNTRUE. I GRADUALLY STOPPED MENTIONING IT AGAIN.

I STILL SUSPECTED THAT HE HADN'T ERASED HIS CHILDHOOD, BUT HAD RATHER SEALED IT
IT IN A BUBBLE, DEEP INSIDE HIS MIND.

INSIDE THAT BUBBLE WAS THE KID WHO'D HAD ALL THOSE ADVENTURES.

IN 1943, THAT KID WAS REGULARLY EXCHANGING BANTER WITH TOP COMEDIANS.

HE MADE GUEST APPEARANCES ON SHOWS LIKE FRED ALLEN'S *TEXACO STAR THEATRE*, DOING SCRIPTED COMEDY.

HE JOKED WITH BOB HOPE, BING CROSBY, JACK BENNY, CHICO MARX. PEOPLE COULDN'T GET ENOUGH OF HIM.

EVERYBODY WANTED TO MEET HIM, AND MY GRANDMOTHER (DESCRIBED BY *THE NEW YORKER* AS A "SMALL, NERVOUS WOMAN") WAS ALWAYS BY HIS SIDE.

SOON HE WAS IN HOLLYWOOD FOR HIS MOVIE DEBUT. HIS SALARY, $2000 A WEEK, WAS BREATHLESSLY REPORTED BY THE NATION'S PRESS.

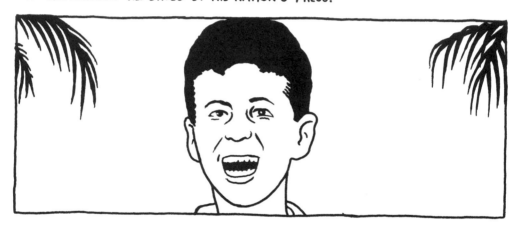

I THINK THIS LATER CONTRIBUTED TO A PERCEPTION THAT HE HAD "MADE A LOT OF MONEY" AS A QUIZ KID.

THE WHOLE FAMILY CAME TO CALIFORNIA WITH JOEL: MOTHER SARA, FATHER SOL, AND SISTER HARRIET.

I'VE REALIZED THAT ONE OF THESE ALBUMS BELONGED TO AUNT HARRIET.

SHE WAS A QUIZ KID TOO, FOR A WHILE.

BOTH THE *QUIZ KID* PRODUCERS AND MY GRANDPARENTS TALKED A LOT ABOUT HOW SHE WAS JUST AS SMART AS MY DAD.

BUT SHE DIDN'T LAST ON THE SHOW, AND EFFORTS TO KEEP HER AS PART OF THE "*QUIZ KIDS* FAMILY" TRAILED OFF.

HER SCRAPBOOK IS ONLY HALF FULL. THE LAST THING IN IT IS A LETTER TO HER FROM THE *QUIZ KIDS* OFFICE.

We want you to know, honey, that we appreciate all you are doing by staying home. You see, by staying home and keeping house you are taking your mother's place...

I THINK THE REASON MY DAD HAD THIS SCRAPBOOK IS BECAUSE SHE DIDN'T WANT IT.

...getting the mail, keeping the house clean, looking after your father. So, you see, she couldn't very well come along, if you weren't so sweet and capable and grown-up.

IN THE UNFINISHED *BECOMING HUMAN*, MY FATHER WROTE:

My sister did not have a chance. I feel guilty every time I see her.

THE MOVIE MY FATHER APPEARED IN WAS CALLED *CHIP OFF THE OLD BLOCK.*
HE PLAYED HIMSELF.

HE'S GOTTEN AWAY FROM HIS PARENTS. HE WANTS TO COME AND STUDY AT THE
NAVAL ACADEMY.

HE MEETS CADET DONALD O'CONNOR, WHO HELPS HIM OUT.

TOGETHER THEY BEFUDDLE A POMPOUS DEAN WHO HASN'T HEARD OF MY DAD.

PRESS REPORTS SUGGEST MY FATHER WAS DIFFICULT TO DIRECT AND HARD TO CONTROL. HE WAS A SEVEN-YEAR-OLD BOY, AFTER ALL.

HE APPEARS TENSE AND UNHAPPY ONSCREEN, DOESN'T SEEM TO KNOW WHAT TO DO WITH HIS HANDS. THERE WERE NO FURTHER MOVIE OFFERS.

IN BETWEEN FILMING HE TOURED THE UNIVERSAL LOT...

...AND DID MATH TRICKS FOR STARS HE DIDN'T RECOGNIZE, SUCH AS MARLENE DIETRICH AND ORSON WELLES.

Miss Dietrich, why don't you call out some numbers, and Joel will add them up!

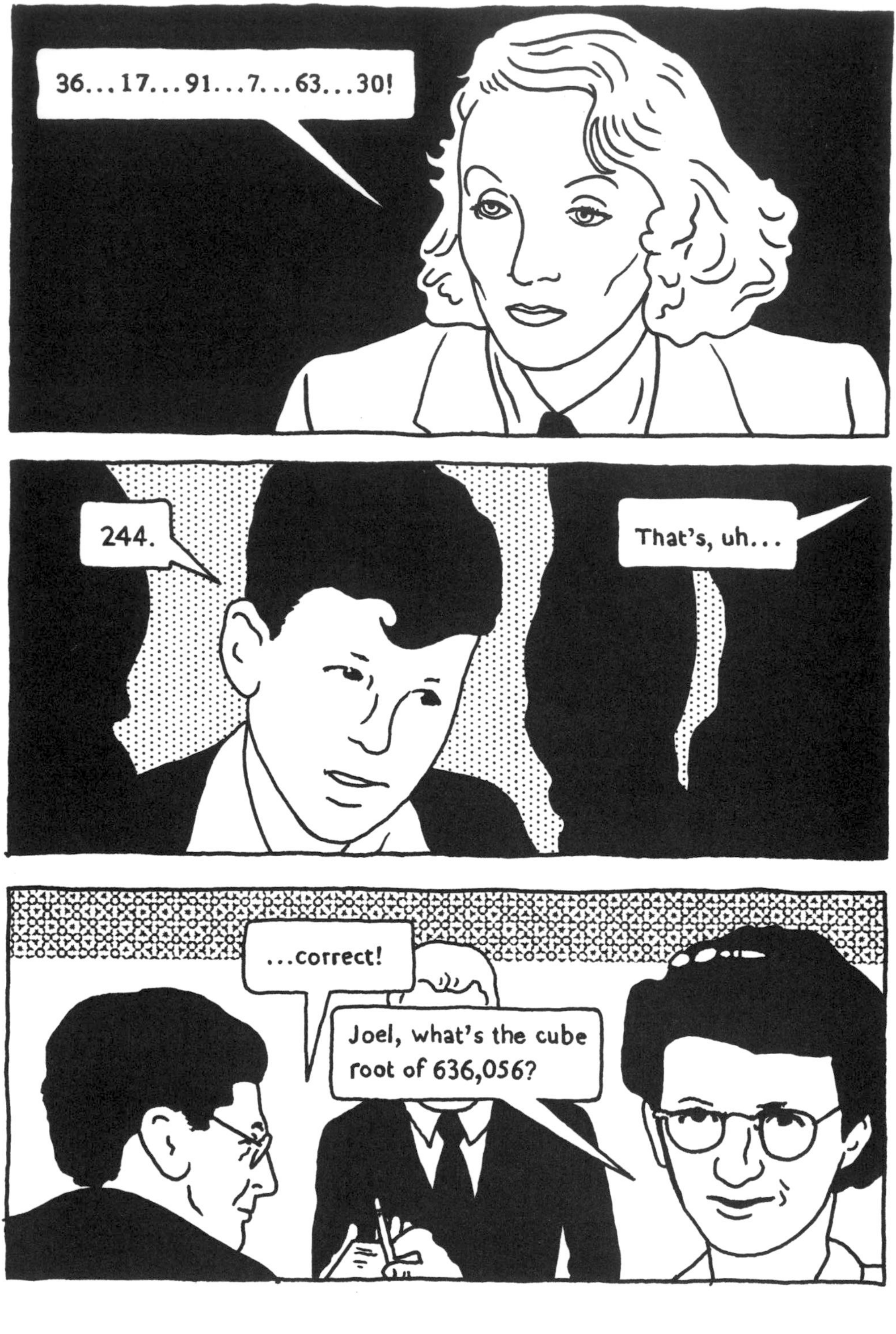
36...17...91...7...63...30!
244.
That's, uh...
...correct!
Joel, what's the cube root of 636,056?

86.

I wish I had him around to help me figure out my income tax. I get so confused!

Joel, let's go meet Orson Welles. He'll do magic for you, won't that be nice?

No!

Hello, Joel, I hear you like magic!

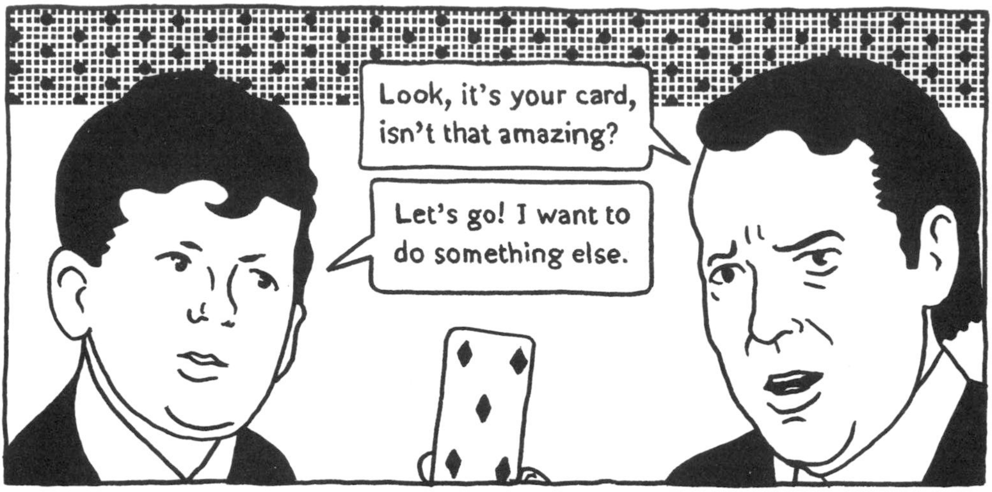
Look, it's your card, isn't that amazing?
Let's go! I want to do something else.

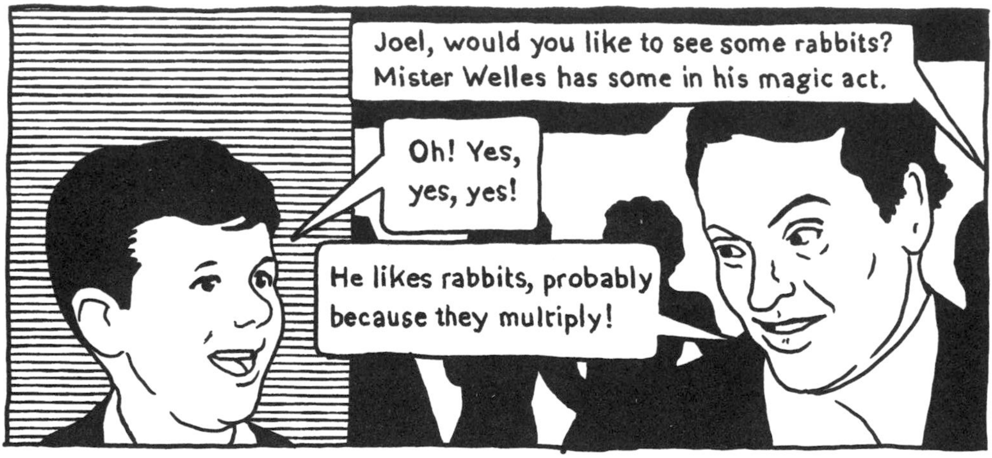
Joel, would you like to see some rabbits? Mister Welles has some in his magic act.
Oh! Yes, yes, yes!
He likes rabbits, probably because they multiply!

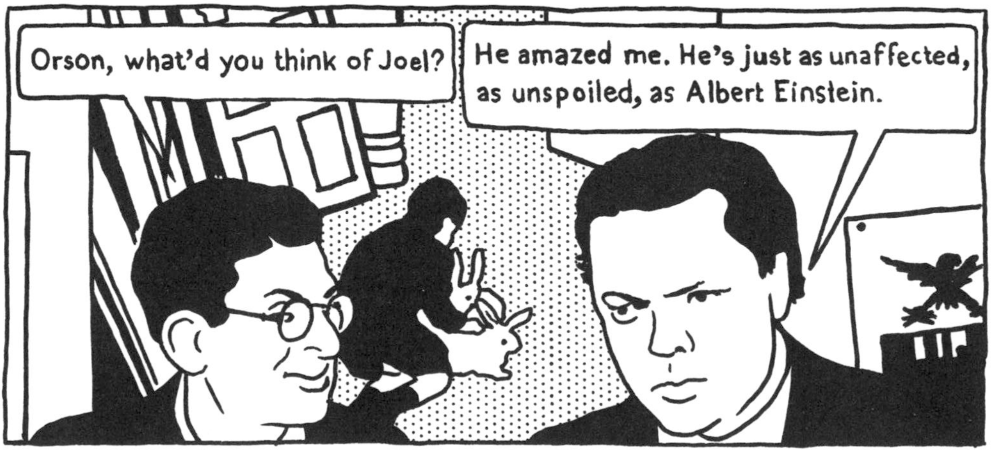
Orson, what'd you think of Joel?
He amazed me. He's just as unaffected, as unspoiled, as Albert Einstein.

A FEW WEEKS LATER, MY DAD APPEARED WITH THE OTHER KIDS AT THE HOLLYWOOD CANTEEN, COMPETING AGAINST FILM STARS SUSAN HAYWARD, JOAN BENNETT, AND JINX FALKENBURG. EDDIE CANTOR WAS THE EMCEE.

MY FATHER DIDN'T KNOW THESE PEOPLE, BUT FOR MY GRANDMOTHER IT MUST HAVE BEEN INCREDIBLE. THEY WERE RIGHT IN THE MIDDLE OF EVERYTHING.

HERE THEY ARE HAVING DINNER AT LINDY'S IN MANHATTAN WITH NEWSPAPERMAN EARL WILSON AND COMEDIAN MILTON BERLE.

...high school!

Joel, sit still.

Joel, I hear you're an income tax expert. Does a taxi ride count as an expense?

If it's used to carry on work, it's deductible.

Joel, wipe your face!

Joel!

Joel!

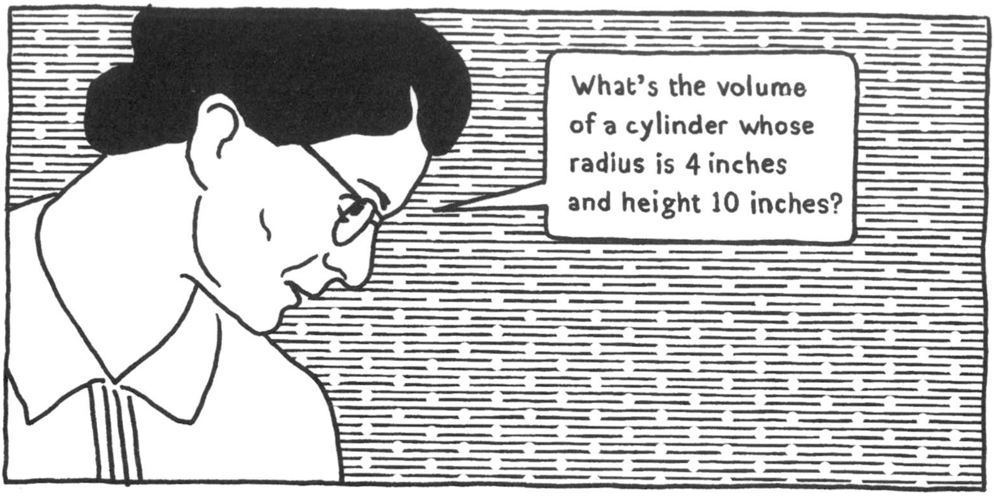
What's the volume of a cylinder whose radius is 4 inches and height 10 inches?

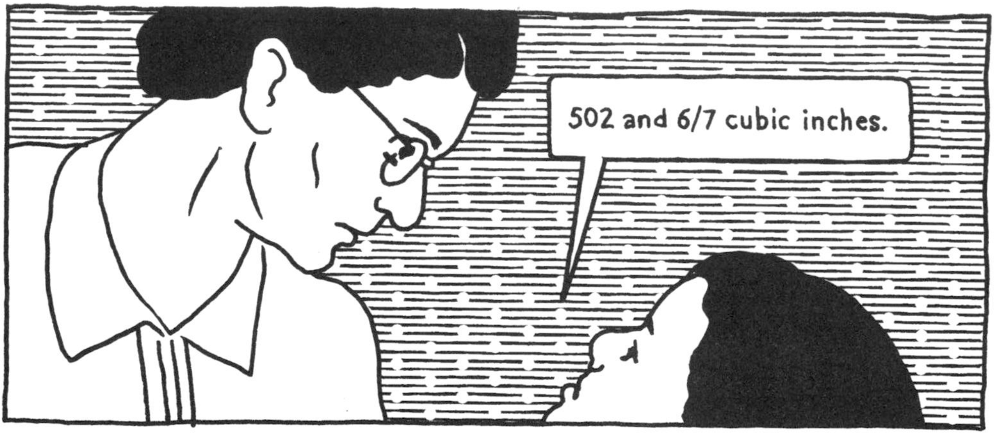
502 and 6/7 cubic inches.

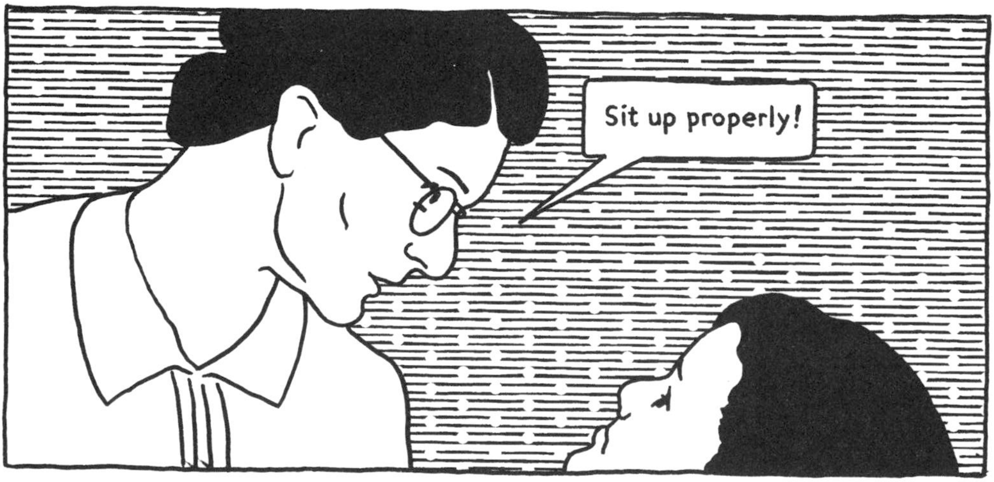
Sit up properly!

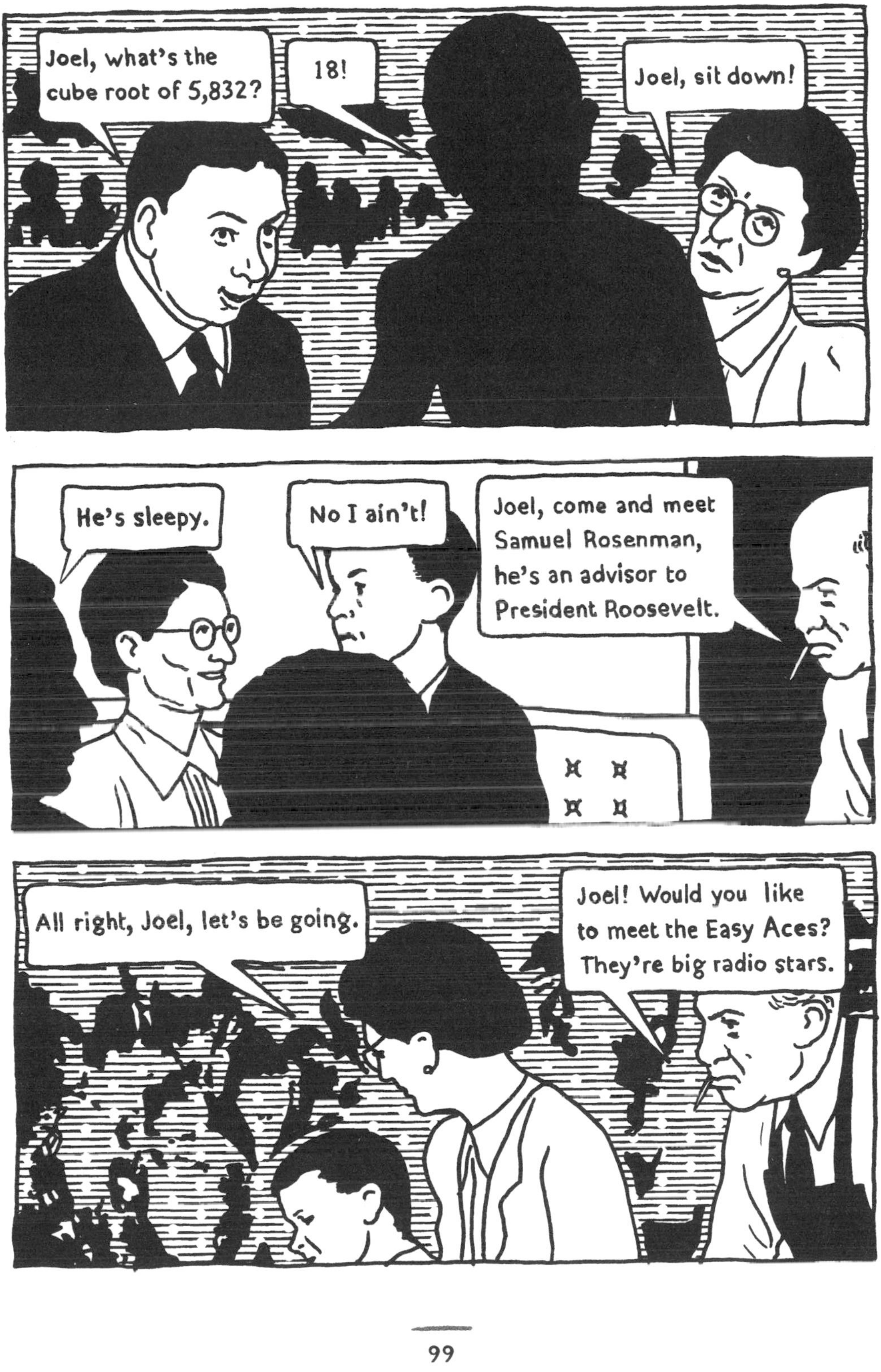
Joel, what's the cube root of 5,832?
18!
Joel, sit down!
He's sleepy.
No I ain't!
Joel, come and meet Samuel Rosenman, he's an advisor to President Roosevelt.
All right, Joel, let's be going.
Joel! Would you like to meet the Easy Aces? They're big radio stars.

CHILDREN ARE VERY EASILY OVERWHELMED. I KNOW THIS NOW AS A FATHER.

THE BRIGHTER AND MORE EXCITABLE A CHILD IS, THE MORE THEY NEED STABILITY AND CONSISTENCY IN THEIR LIVES.

MY FATHER WAS GETTING THE OPPOSITE.

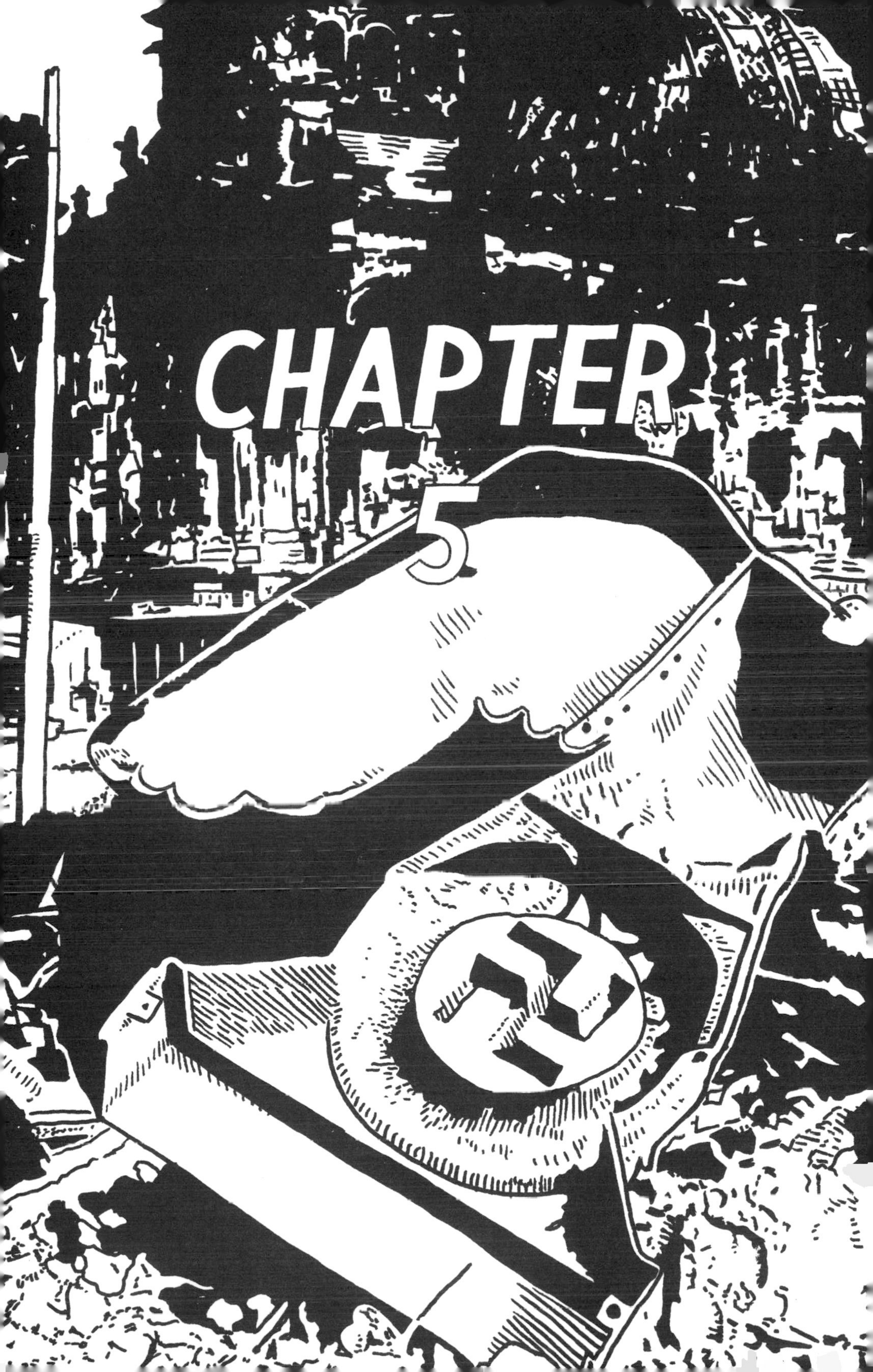
CHAPTER
5

I can't even look at [Charles Schumer] without being reminded of an old radio-and-television show called *Quiz Kids*, which featured a boy genius named Joel Kupperman who was always waving his hand wildly whenever a question was asked and shouting, "I know! I know!"

—Nora Ephron in *The Huffington Post*, 2007

WORLD WAR II LENT EVERYTHING DRAMA AND PURPOSE.

AMERICANS WERE MORE UNITED THAN THEY EVER HAD BEEN OR WOULD BE AGAIN. LINKED TOGETHER IN A COMMON CAUSE: DEFEATING EVIL.

THE *QUIZ KID* STARS TOURED CONSTANTLY, MAKING APPEARANCES IN NEW YORK, PHILADELPHIA, HOUSTON, HOLLYWOOD, DETROIT, SAN FRANCISCO, PITTSBURGH, CINCINNATI, INDIANAPOLIS, BOSTON, FORT WAYNE, NEW ORLEANS, MEMPHIS, BATON ROUGE, OMAHA, SEATTLE, VANCOUVER, PORTLAND, SALT LAKE CITY, LAFAYETTE (IN), TOPEKA, HARTFORD, WASHINGTON DC, DALLAS, BUFFALO, PEORIA, SPRINGFIELD (IL), DES MOINES, AND CLEVELAND. BY THE END OF THE WAR THEY'D SOLD $125 MILLION WORTH OF BONDS.

Children, our first question is from Nathan Weintraub of Camden, New Jersey. . .

. . .how many miles are we from Berlin. Harve?

The last report I heard was that we were nearing 21 miles from Berlin.

Well, we have some other hands up. Ruthie?

Well I think one of our armies is within 90 miles, but I don't know.

WHILE THE WAR EXPANDED SOME INDUSTRIES, IT HAD HALTED DEVELOPMENT IN OTHERS, LIKE TELEVISION. WITH PEACE IN SIGHT, WORK ON TV WAS RESUMING.

A MONTH EARLIER, THE KIDS HAD BEEN IN NEW YORK AS PART OF A NIGHT OF TV BROADCASTING FOR THEIR NEW NETWORK, ABC.

THE QUIZ KIDS, WEARING DARK CLOTHES IN FRONT OF A DARK BACKGROUND, WERE PART OF A LINEUP THAT INCLUDED SHOWS CALLED *LADIES BE SEATED* AND *ON STAGE, EVERYBODY.*

ONLY A HANDFUL OF PEOPLE SAW IT. IT WAS CRUDE AND AMATEURISH. STILL, IT WAS CONSIDERED A SUCCESS. ABC TOUTED THE BROADCAST IN BROCHURES TO INVESTORS, AND TV MANUFACTURERS DUMONT FEATURED THE KIDS IN ADS.

FOR NOW, TV WAS ONLY ON IN A FEW CITIES, FOR A FEW HOURS. THE REST OF AMERICA WAS GOING TO HAVE TO WAIT.

THE WAR IN EUROPE ENDED IN MAY. THE WAR IN JAPAN ENDED IN AUGUST WITH THE ATOMIC BOMB DROPPED ON THE JAPANESE CITIES OF HIROSHIMA AND NAGASAKI.

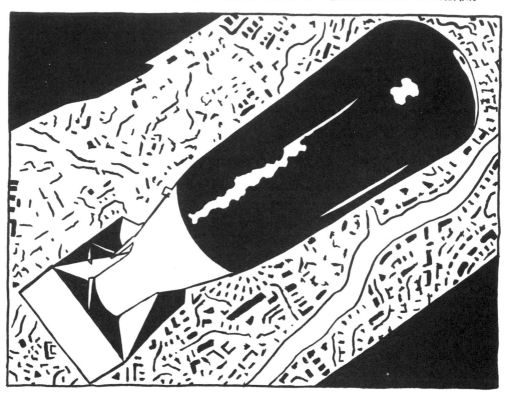

GLENN SEABORG, ONE OF THE PHYSICISTS WHO HAD WORKED ON THE BOMB, APPEARED ON *QUIZ KIDS* TO EXPLAIN THE NEW REALITY.

The whole downtown of Chicago, including the Merchandise Mart where we are now, could be vaporized by one atomic bomb...

While the judges add up the scores, I'd like to tell you about a little boy who grew up in Czechoslovakia. David Hoffman is his name.

When David was seven years old, the Nazis took David and his family to the concentration camp at Auschwitz, where this little boy saw his parents and brothers and sisters cremated.

David escaped, but he was recaptured and sent to the horror camp at Dachau. When the American army liberated Dachau, they found David, starved and dirty.

The Red Cross took David and nursed him back to health. They located another sister and brought David to her here in America.

He's a guest in our classroom right now, attending his very first broadcast, and he has a short message for you. Go ahead, David.

Just want to say that I hope everyone will give to the Red Cross.

WHEN THE UNITED NATIONS HELD ITS FIRST ASSEMBLY IN NEW YORK CITY, MY FATHER WAS INVITED TO SPEAK AS THE REPRESENTATIVE OF AMERICAN YOUTH. THE *QUIZ KIDS* OFFICE HELPED HIM CRAFT HIS SPEECH.

MY FATHER SAT IN ON THE SESSIONS, BUT QUICKLY LOST INTEREST.

WITH THE WAR OVER, *QUIZ KIDS* NEEDED A NEW WAY TO JUSTIFY ITSELF. THE SHOW HAD TO BE ABOUT A CAUSE, NOT JUST KIDS ANSWERING QUESTIONS.

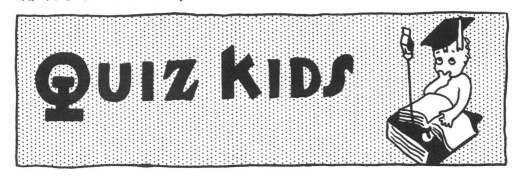

SO IT BECAME *EDUCATIONAL*.

THE SHOW STARTED A "TEACHER OF THE YEAR" CONTEST AND ENCOURAGED KIDS ALL OVER THE COUNTRY TO NOMINATE THEIR TEACHERS. IT WAS WILDLY SUCCESSFUL. PROMINENT EXPERTS AND POLITICIANS OFFERED RINGING ENDORSEMENTS OF "THE MOST EDUCATIONAL SHOW ON RADIO."

THIS WAS A MISREPRESENTATION. THE SHOW WAS NOT EDUCATIONAL AT ALL. NOBODY EVER LEARNED ANYTHING FROM *QUIZ KIDS*. IT WAS A TRIVIA CONTEST.

NOW IT WAS ASPIRATIONAL. YOU, TOO, COULD BE A QUIZ KID, IF YOU STUDIED HARD AND PAID ATTENTION. LOCAL CHAPTERS SPRANG UP AROUND THE COUNTRY.

BEFORE, MY FATHER HAD BEEN AN UNPRECEDENTED PRODIGY WHO DISRUPTED CLASS BY STARTLING HIS ILL-PREPARED TEACHERS. NOW HE WAS A GOOD EXAMPLE, A KID WHO LISTENED AND STUDIED HARD. A ROLE MODEL.

THIS IS WHEN MOST ORDINARY KIDS STARTED TO HATE HIM.

HARVE AND RICHARD REACHED THE "GRADUATION AGE" OF SIXTEEN AND LEFT THE SHOW. RUTHIE CHOSE TO STEP AWAY, RETURNING VERY OCCASIONALLY.

MY FATHER STAYED ON.

THROUGH HIS ENTIRE CHILDHOOD.

HAVING JOINED THE SHOW WHEN HE WAS SO YOUNG, I THINK HE ABSORBED THE LESSON THAT ANSWERING QUESTIONS WAS HIS JOB. MY FATHER WAS NEVER A QUITTER.

THE IDEA THAT THE SHOW WAS "EDUCATIONAL," THAT DISPLAYING KNOWLEDGE WAS AN HONORABLE THING TO DO, BLINDED MY FATHER AND HIS FAMILY AS TO WHAT WAS ACTUALLY HAPPENING.

MY FATHER WAS IN SHOW BUSINESS, A CONTESTANT ON A NEVER-ENDING GAME SHOW WITH NO PRIZES. AND HE WAS OVERSTAYING HIS WELCOME.

IN WOODY ALLEN'S *RADIO DAYS*, THERE'S A RADIO MATH WHIZ WHO IS DEFINITELY MODELED ON MY FATHER.

HE'S A SNOTTY, CONDESCENDING CREEP WHO SNEERS AT ORDINARY PEOPLE.

PEOPLE WERE GETTING TIRED OF HIM.

WHY COULDN'T HE QUIT? WHEN I'D ASKED HIM EARLIER HE'D SAID:

Money was a factor... it was $75 a week...

Did you tell your parents you were feeling uncomfortable with the show?

Oh, they knew it. Yes. Yes.

But they said you should stay on?

Well, they didn't say it...

...but I think they assumed it, and I wasn't a rebellious kid... I was willing to go along...

Do you wish you had rebelled?

Not particularly. I mean, what good would it have done?

You could have said, "I'm not doing the show anymore."

Yeah, but it didn't hurt me that much, you know... I was a little uncomfortable, that's all...

NOW THAT I CAN SEE THE LEVEL OF DENIAL, IT'S INCREDIBLE. THE TRAUMA HAS BECOME ALMOST VISIBLE TO ME AS A NEGATIVE SHAPE.

THE GAPING HOLE IN MY FATHER'S MEMORIES. THERE *BEFORE* THE DEMENTIA.

HE REMEMBERED THE LEAST ABOUT THE TIMES THAT HURT HIM THE MOST.

HE REMEMBERED ABSOLUTELY NOTHING ABOUT BEING ON TV.

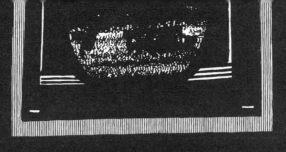

CHAPTER

6

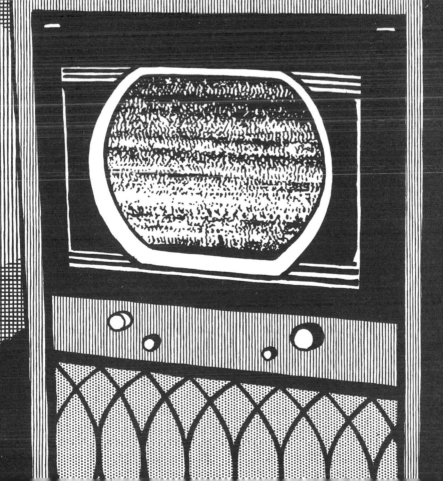

The biggest kid star in both radio and TV was Joel Kupperman, who was ten and had an IQ over 200. He answered algebra problems almost instantly with no pencil or paper. His amazing math skills had radio listeners worried that *Quiz Kids* might be fixed. It wasn't until they saw Kupperman on the TV version that viewers were convinced of his honesty.

—Michael Ritchie,
Please Stand By: A Prehistory of Television

EVERYONE AGREES: MY GRANDMOTHER WAS AN EXCEPTIONALLY AGGRESSIVE AND DETERMINED STAGE MOTHER.

SHE WOULD USE ANY PSYCHOLOGICAL TACTIC SHE COULD TO KEEP HER SON IN SHOW BUSINESS, DESPITE THE FACT THAT HE WAS INCREASINGLY OBVIOUSLY UNSUITED TO IT.

BY THE END OF 1948, HE WAS ENTERING AN AWKWARD ADOLESCENCE. HIS VOICE THICKENED, HE GREW TALLER AND MORE SELF-CONSCIOUS. HE SMILED LESS. NO LONGER WAS HE THE CUTE KID WHO HAD ENCHANTED AMERICA.

MANY KIDS HATED HIM BY NOW, BUT THEY DIDN'T KNOW WHAT HE LOOKED LIKE. ALL THEY KNEW WAS THE VOICE.

TIME FOR HIM TO BE A TV STAR.

TV GREW SLOWLY. *QUIZ KIDS* BECAME A TV SHOW IN JANUARY 1949, BUT ONLY IN CHICAGO. STATIONS WERE ADDED GRADUALLY UNTIL, A YEAR LATER, IT WAS BEING BROADCAST ON THE NEW, NATIONAL NBC NETWORK, FRIDAY NIGHTS, 8 PM.

MILTON BERLE HAD BECOME THE FIRST BIG TV STAR. HE GUESTED ON *QUIZ KIDS* IN JANUARY 1950, AND THE KIDS WERE ON HIS SHOW TWO DAYS LATER.

MY FATHER SEEMED TO GENUINELY ENJOY HORSING AROUND WITH HIM.

IN EVERY OTHER SURVIVING CLIP OF THE SHOW, MY FATHER IS A GRIM NERD WHO ONLY CARES ABOUT DOING HIS JOB. ANSWERING QUESTIONS.

HIS HAND IS ALWAYS UP. IF THE FIRST QUESTION IS ASKED BEFORE THE CREDITS, HIS HAND STAYS UP THROUGH THE CREDITS, SOMETIMES OBSCURING ANOTHER KID'S FACE.

IT DOESN'T MAKE FOR RIVETING TV.

Here's tonight's first question...

GUEST HOST
FRAN ALLISON

If I take a cup of coffee, and transfer it to this cup of milk, then stir it up...

...and take a cup of that mixture, and put it in the jar of coffee...

...will I have transferred more coffee to the milk jar, or more milk to the coffee jar? Joel?

Well, say there are x cups in either the, uh, coffee or milk, so when you take out one cup of the coffee to the milk...

...there are x+1 cups in the milk, and of those x+1 cups, x are coffee and 1 is of, uh, milk. So when you transfer a cup back, of that cup, uh, uh...

...1 over x+1 will be of, uh, coffee, while x over x+1 will be of milk. So if you take the 1 over x+1...

...away from the 1, you get x over x+1 cups of coffee left in the milk and you have that milk in coffee, so...

...it would come out even.

Very good, Joel!

TO BALANCE MY DAD, THE SHOW TRIED PUTTING SMALLER AND CUTER CHILDREN NEXT TO HIM, BILLED AS "NURSERY RHYME EXPERTS" OR WHATEVER.

THEY TRIED EVERYTHING TO MAKE IT FUN OR INTERESTING. THEY HYPNOTIZED HIM.

Whenever I ask you what five and five is, you will say that it is twelve!

Five and five is twelve! Five and five is twelve!

THEY HAD HIM DO MATH WHILE TAKING A DRIVING TEST, OR WHILE RIDING A TINY LOCOMOTIVE. THEY BROUGHT IN OUTSIDERS TO COMPETE.

On the mechanical side, we have an adding machine and an abacus. On the human side, our very own Joel Kupperman!

NOTHING WORKED. NO ONE CARED ANYMORE. PEOPLE WERE TIRED OF *QUIZ KIDS.*

Well folks, Joel has no paper or pencil, he just has to use his head on this, but he's looking mighty aler—

CLICK

IN 1952, HE WAS TURNING SIXTEEN, THE SHOW'S "GRADUATION AGE." BUT AN ANNOUNCEMENT APPEARED IN THE PRESS SAYING THAT HE WAS "EXEMPT" FROM THE AGE LIMIT AND WOULD CONTINUE TO APPEAR.

THE SHOW DIDN'T WANT TO LET HIM GO. HIS MOTHER DIDN'T WANT IT TO END.

THAT JUNE, LOUIS G. COWAN THREW A HUGE PARTY TO MARK THE TWELFTH ANNIVERSARY OF THE SHOW. MORE THAN FOUR HUNDRED QUIZ KIDS, PAST AND PRESENT, WERE INVITED.

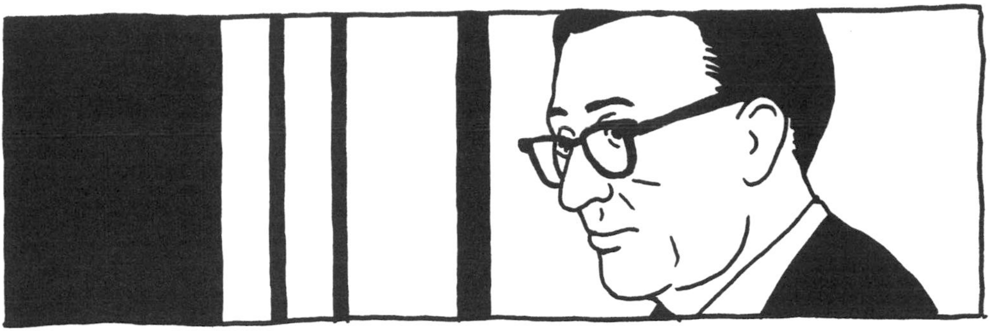

MY DAD HAD GRADUATED HIGH SCHOOL AND WAS SET TO ATTEND UNIVERSITY OF CHICAGO, STAYING CLOSE TO HIS PARENTS. STILL APPEARING ON THE SHOW.

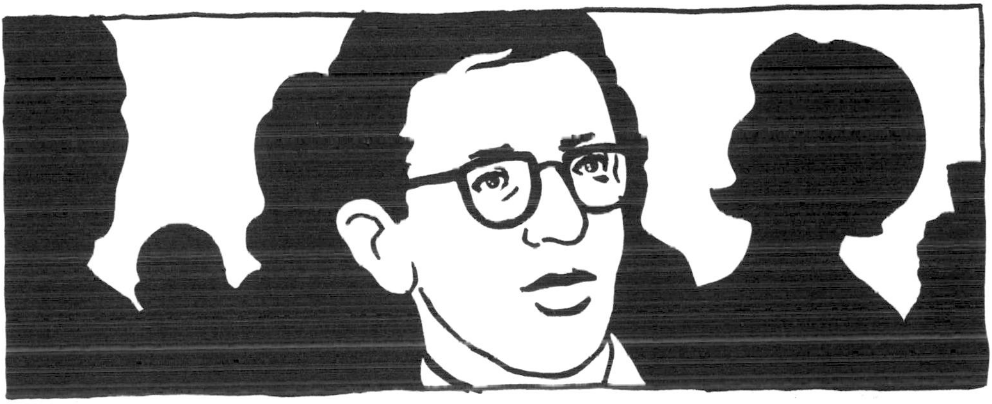

WHAT MUST THAT NIGHT HAVE BEEN LIKE FOR HIM? EVERYONE ELSE HAD MOVED ON. THEY'D MARRIED, GOTTEN JOBS, HAD CHILDREN. ENTERED THE REAL WORLD.

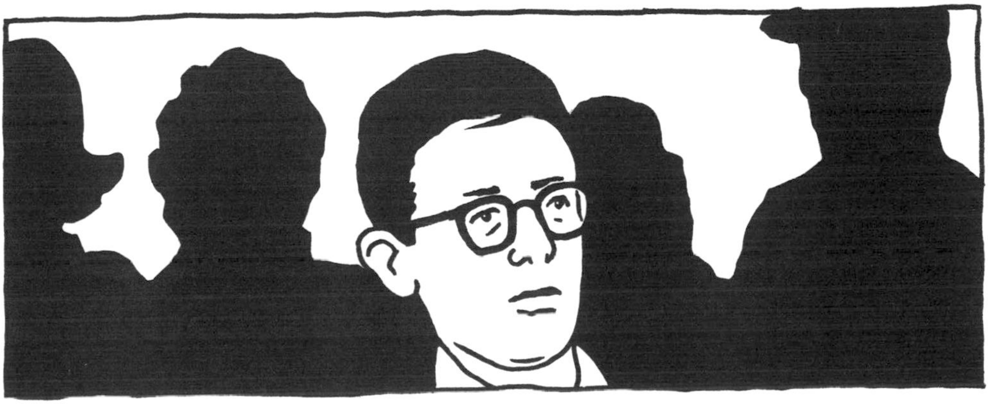

MAYBE THAT WAS THE NIGHT HE FINALLY SAID "ENOUGH."

MAYBE THAT WAS WHEN HE FINALLY STOOD UP TO HIS MOTHER.

I KNOW IT HAPPENED. EVEN IF HE BLOTTED IT FROM HIS MEMORY LONG AGO. IT HAPPENED. IT HAS TO HAVE.

BECAUSE HE LEFT THE SHOW. I DON'T KNOW EXACTLY WHEN. HE WAS ON IT AND THEN HE WASN'T.

HIS CAREER ON *QUIZ KIDS* HAD STARTED WITH HUGE FANFARE. AND ENDED WITH NONE. HE HAD BEEN ON *QUIZ KIDS* FOR MORE THAN TEN YEARS. AROUND FOUR HUNDRED EPISODES ON RADIO AND TV.

NOW HE WAS FREE. JUST AN ORDINARY PERSON AGAIN. HIS CHILDHOOD BEHIND HIM.

BUT THE PAST WASN'T DONE WITH HIM.

You were still getting recognized a lot?

Yeah. Yeah. Kids my age who hated me.

I developed all sorts of defense mechanisms against this hostility. It was very difficult to deal with.

Because you'd been used as an example for them?

Probably... well, in some cases they said that!

I CAN'T IMAGINE HOW BAD THE NEXT FEW YEARS WERE FOR HIM. BUT I'VE FOUND A DESCRIPTION ONLINE OF HOW HE WAS BULLIED (BY ONE OF THE BULLIES).

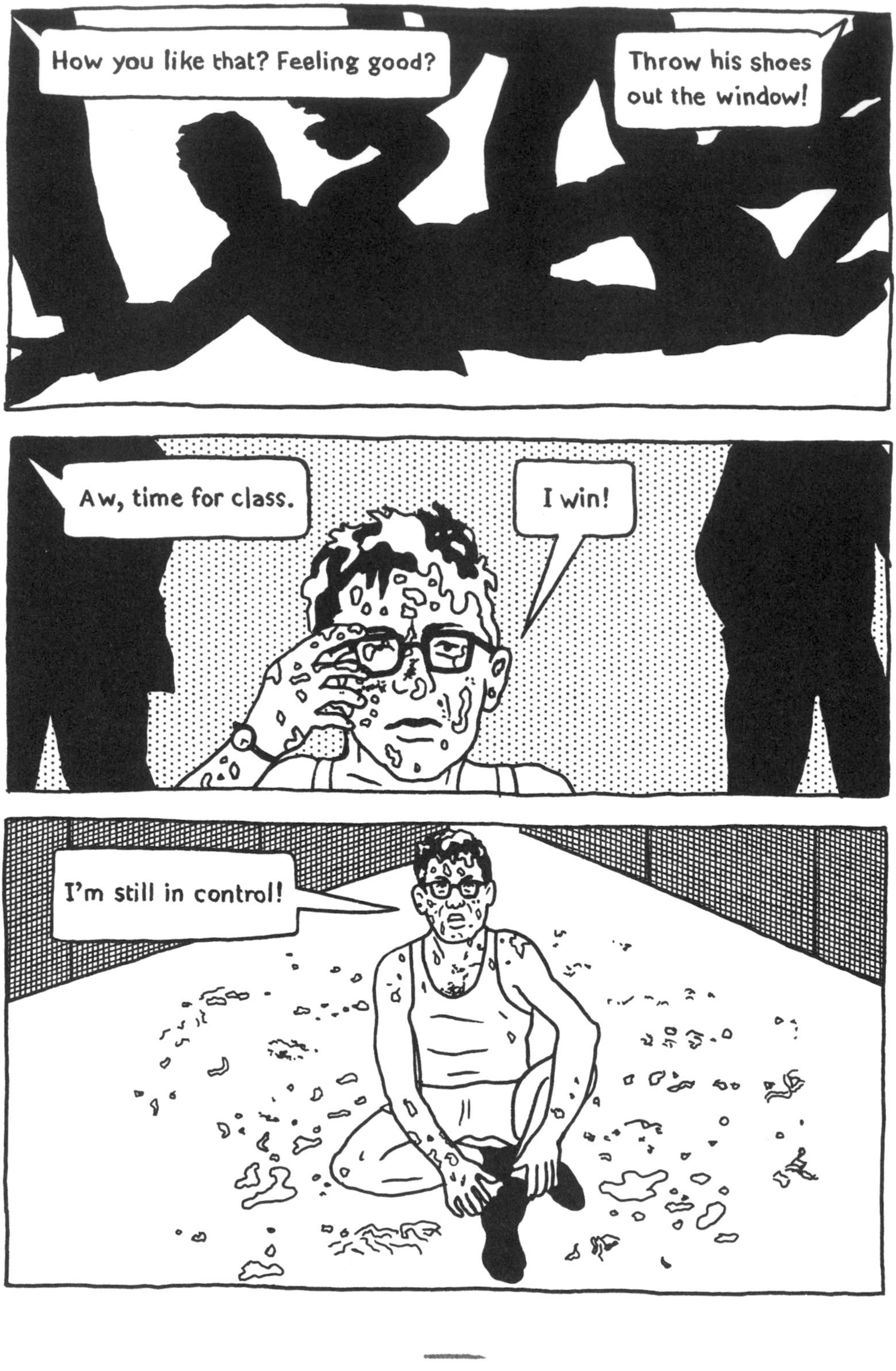
How you like that? Feeling good?
Throw his shoes out the window!
Aw, time for class.
I win!
I'm still in control!

TOWARD THE END OF HIS TIME AT THE UNIVERSITY, A VISITING PROFESSOR SAID SOMETHING TO HIM. IT WAS A BIG MOMENT FOR MY FATHER. HE STILL REMEMBERED IT AND DESCRIBED IT WITH GENUINE WONDER SIXTY YEARS LATER.

THIS IDEA HAD NEVER OCCURRED TO HIM.

HE COULD LEAVE IT ALL BEHIND. HE COULD GO STUDY IN CAMBRIDGE, ENGLAND.

HE COULD BE ANONYMOUS.

LEARN TO BE A REAL PERSON.

I WISH I COULD GO BACK THROUGH THE DECADES.

GO ACROSS THE OCEAN.

FIND HIM IN CAMBRIDGE.

GRAB HIM BY THE LAPELS AND SHOUT INTO HIS STUPID, CONFUSED FACE:

DON'T COME BACK!!!

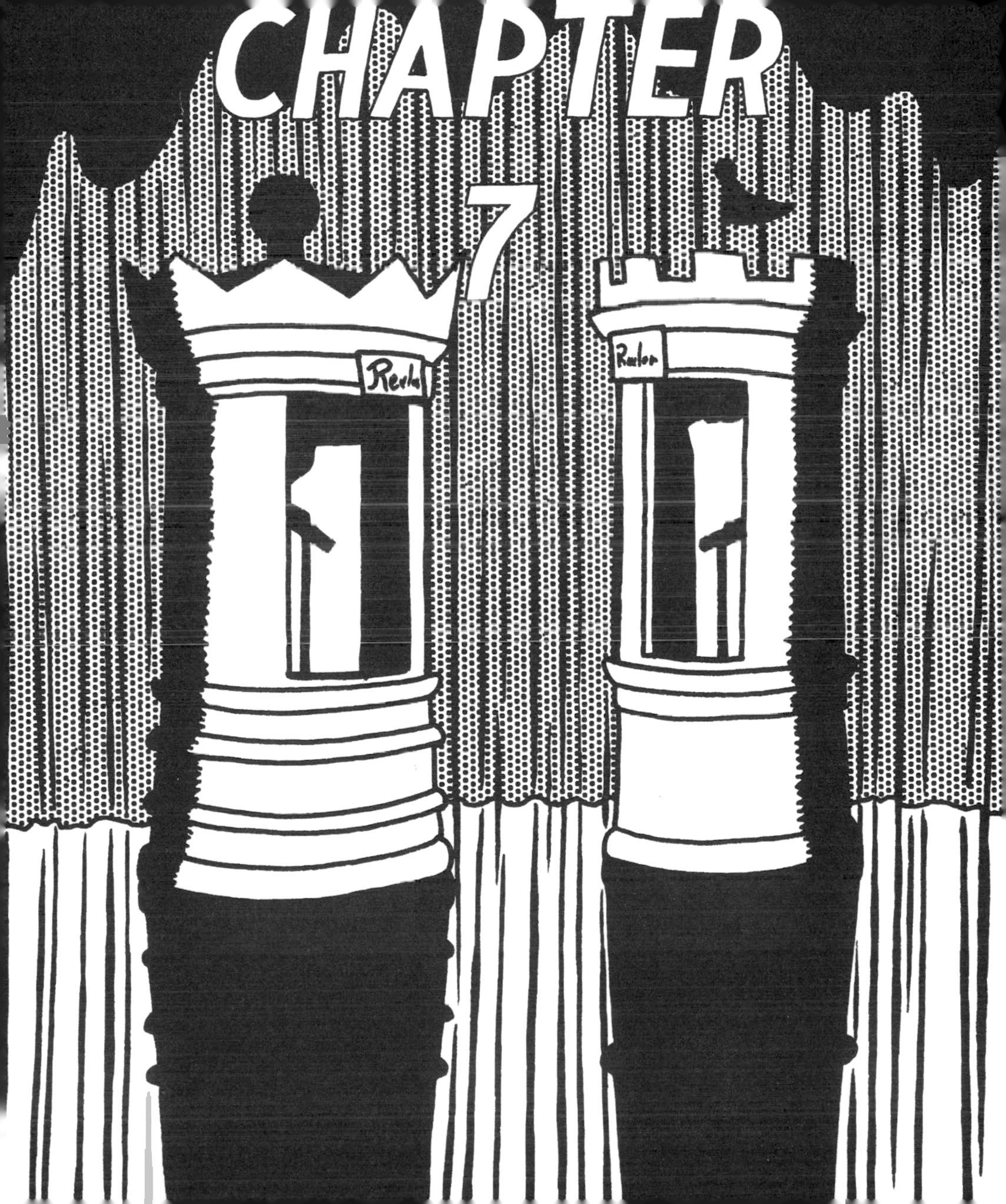
CHAPTER
7

The greatest thing television has to offer is reality... watching the real thing, with no predetermined outcome.

—Louis G. Cowan

IN THE SUMMER OF 1957, MY FATHER RETURNED TO AMERICA FOR A VISIT.

SOMEONE, ALMOST CERTAINLY HIS MOTHER, ARRANGED FOR HIM TO BE ON A GAME SHOW THAT WAS HEAVILY RIGGED.

SHE STILL THOUGHT HE BELONGED ON TV.

LOUIS G. COWAN HAD STAYED BUSY. HE SAW POSSIBILITIES IN TV NO ONE ELSE DID. IN 1955 HE'D BEEN THINKING ABOUT MOUNT EVEREST AND GAME SHOWS.

WHAT IF CONTESTANTS CLIMBED A MOUNTAIN... OF MONEY?

MOUNTAINEERS MADE BASE CAMPS IN BETWEEN STRETCHES OF CLIMBING. WHAT IF...

WHAT IF CONTESTANTS KEPT COMING BACK, AND PLAYING FOR HIGHER STAKES, BUT RISKED LOSING WHAT THEY HAD ALREADY WON?

THE SHOW COWAN DEVISED, *THE $64,000 QUESTION*, WAS A MASSIVE SUCCESS THAT TRANSFORMED THE FACE OF TV.

THIS WAS THE NEW FEVER DREAM OF AMERICA. APPEAR ON A GAME SHOW FOR A FEW NIGHTS, WIN AN INCREDIBLE AMOUNT OF MONEY, BECOME FAMOUS.

ROBERT STROM, AN ELEVEN-YEAR-OLD FROM THE BRONX, WON $224,000 APPEARING ON *QUESTION* AND ITS SISTER SHOW, *THE $64,000 CHALLENGE*.

BIG-MONEY GAME SHOWS SPRANG UP LIKE MUSHROOMS: *DOTTO, TWENTY ONE, THE BIG SURPRISE, TIC TAC DOUGH, DOUGH RE MI, TREASURE HUNT, PLAY YOUR HUNCH, ANYBODY CAN WIN, PICK A WINNER*, AND MORE.

COWAN, NOW OFFICIALLY A GENIUS, WAS HIRED BY CBS, AND WITHIN A YEAR HE WAS PRESIDENT OF THEIR TV DIVISION.

HE BELIEVED IN TV AS AN ARTISTIC MEDIUM. HE CHAMPIONED SHOWS LIKE *CAPTAIN KANGAROO* AND *THE TWILIGHT ZONE*.

BUT HE HAD SEWN THE SEEDS OF HIS OWN DOWNFALL. THE GAME SHOWS HAD QUICKLY DESCENDED INTO CORRUPTION AND TRICKERY.

SPONSORS HAD BEGUN DEMANDING THE RIGHT TO CHOOSE WHO WON AND WHO LOST. THEY WANTED WINNERS WHO RESEMBLED THE KIND OF PEOPLE THEY WERE SELLING TO.

SOON MOST SHOWS WERE RIGGED. IT WAS AN OPEN SECRET AMONG THE SMART SET. ONLY AVERAGE AMERICANS DIDN'T KNOW.

MY FATHER HAD NO IDEA WHEN HE WENT TO NEW YORK IN JULY TO APPEAR ON *THE $64,000 CHALLENGE,* ONE OF THE MOST RIGGED SHOWS ON TV.

IN AN INTERVIEW WITH THE *NEW YORK POST* (THE LAST HE EVER GAVE), MY FATHER SEEMS CONFIDENT AND RELAXED.

HE'S DOING THE SHOW FOR THE MONEY, HE TELLS THE REPORTER, BECAUSE HE "ONLY MADE $18,000 ON *QUIZ KIDS*."

OBVIOUSLY HE'D ACCEPTED THAT ALL HE NEEDED TO DO WAS WHAT HE HAD ALWAYS DONE: ANSWER QUESTIONS. BUT THIS TIME HE WOULD MAKE BIG MONEY.

THE CLASSIC AMERICAN SETUP FOR TRAGEDY.

PEOPLE HAD ALWAYS ASKED IF *QUIZ KIDS* WAS RIGGED. IN FACT, THE PRODUCERS HAD SUGGESTED BOOKS FOR MY FATHER TO READ, AND THEY HAD TAILORED THE QUESTIONS TO HIS ABILITIES.

BUT HE HAD ANSWERED ALL THE QUESTIONS USING HIS OWN MENTAL POWER, AND HAD NEVER KNOWN WHAT THEY WERE BEFOREHAND. IN HIS MIND, HE HAD ALWAYS BEEN HONEST.

SO WHAT HAPPENED NEXT HURT HIM, AND IT HAUNTED HIM FOR THE REST OF HIS LIFE.

YEARS AGO HE'D TOLD MY MOTHER ABOUT HOW IT HAPPENED. USING HER MEMORIES OF WHAT HE'D SAID, AND MY OWN RESEARCH INTO HOW THE SHOWS OPERATED, I'VE CONSTRUCTED A VERSION OF HOW IT WENT.

The $64,000 CHALLENGE

MY FATHER'S FIRST APPEARANCE ON *CHALLENGE* WENT SMOOTHLY. THEY ASKED HIM A QUESTION, HE ANSWERED IT. AND THEN HE WAS SCHEDULED FOR THE NEXT SHOW.

THE WORD CAME DOWN TO THE *CHALLENGE* PRODUCERS: MAKE SURE HE ANSWERS HIS NEXT QUESTION CORRECTLY. WE WANT THE QUIZ KID TO CONTINUE WINNING.

THESE PEOPLE WERE VERY CUNNING. THEY WOULDN'T GIVE HIM THE ANSWERS DIRECTLY; THEY'D ARRANGE FOR ANOTHER CONTESTANT TO DO IT. SOMEWHERE AWAY FROM THE OFFICES, IF POSSIBLE. MAKE IT LOOK LIKE COINCIDENCE OR LUCK.

MAYBE THEY'D ASKED MY DAD TO COME IN EARLY BEFORE THE SECOND SHOW AND FILL OUT SOME PAPERWORK. WHILE HE'S THERE, THEY INTRODUCE HIM TO ANOTHER CONTESTANT.

MAYBE THEY SUGGEST THE TWO MEN HAVE COFFEE TOGETHER, TO KILL TIME BEFORE THE BROADCAST.

There's a fascinating chapter about operas with famous choruses. *Faust* and the, uh...

Soldier's Chorus.

Yes! And Wagner's *Tannhauser* with the...

Pilgrim's Chorus.

Of course *Il Trovatore* has the...

Anvil Chorus.

THE *$64,000 CHALLENGE* TAKES PLACE ON A SET DOMINATED BY TWO HUGE CHESS PIECES, WHICH CONTAIN THE ISOLATION BOOTHS.

MY FATHER IS ESCORTED ON BY A MODEL AND EXCHANGES SOME BANTER WITH THE HOST, RALPH STORY.

Joel, back for your second night. Feeling lucky?

THEN HE'S PLACED IN ONE OF THE BOOTHS DURING THE LENGTHY AD FOR KENT CIGARETTES.

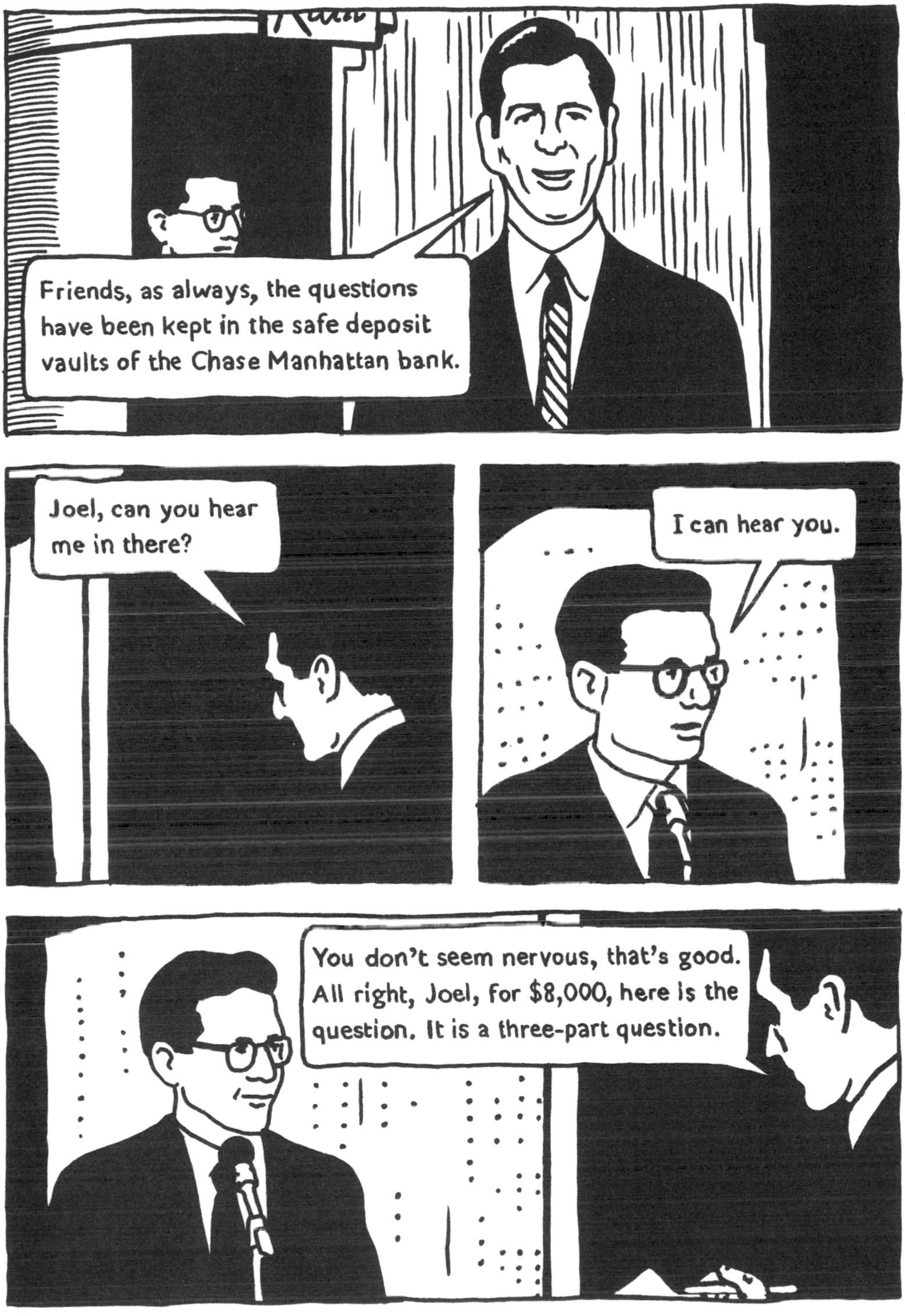
Friends, as always, the questions have been kept in the safe deposit vaults of the Chase Manhattan bank.
Joel, can you hear me in there?
I can hear you.
You don't seem nervous, that's good. All right, Joel, for $8,000, here is the question. It is a three-part question.

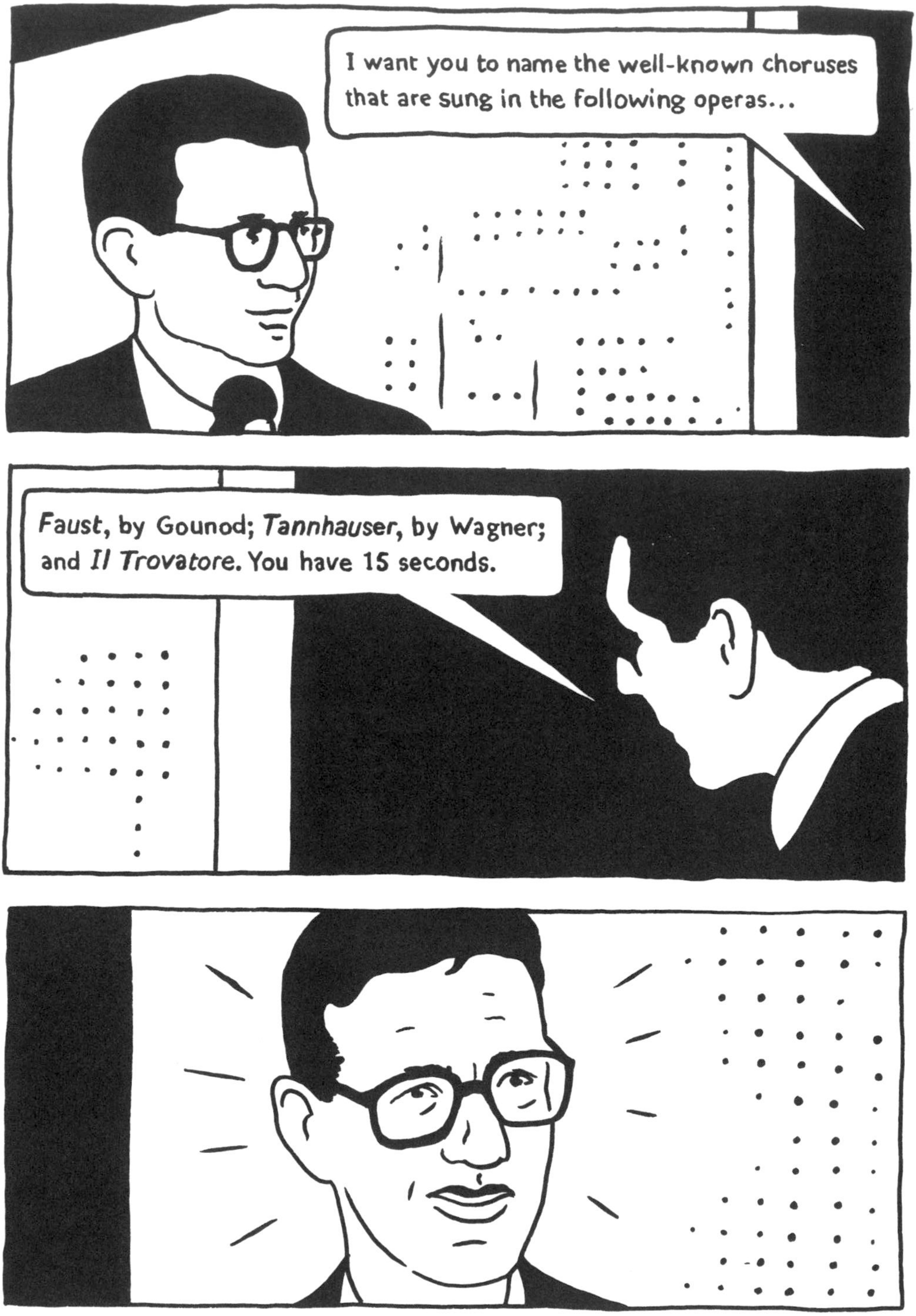
I want you to name the well-known choruses that are sung in the following operas...
Faust, by Gounod; *Tannhauser*, by Wagner; and *Il Trovatore*. You have 15 seconds.

THE TRAP SNAPS SHUT ON HIM LIVE ON NATIONAL TV.

HE WOULD HAVE ANSWERED THE QUESTION—HE DID KNOW THE ANSWERS, AFTER ALL, FAIR AND SQUARE—AND THAT WAS HIS JOB, ANSWERING QUESTIONS.

BUT HE WOULD ALWAYS FEEL THAT HE'D PARTICIPATED IN SOMETHING DISHONEST.

161

MY FATHER WASN'T THE TYPE TO MAKE WAVES. HE FINISHED THE SHOW AND WALKED AWAY AFTER TELLING THEM HE WOULDN'T BE BACK. I'M SURE HE LEFT ANGRY, AND MAYBE THEY TRIED TO MAKE SURE HE WASN'T GOING TO SAY ANYTHING. BUT HE'D JUST WANT TO LEAVE. JUST WANT TO GET AWAY.

HE TRIED TO PUSH THE SHAME DOWN AND FORGET IT. BUT IT ATE AWAY AT HIM.

AND HE SPENT THE NEXT FIFTY YEARS THINKING ABOUT CHARACTER, ETHICS, MORALITY.

TWO YEARS AFTER MY FATHER'S LAST APPEARANCE ON TV, THE DISHONESTY OF TELEVISION WAS FINALLY EXPOSED TO A SHOCKED PUBLIC.

I think I share the American general reaction of almost bewilderment that people could conspire to confuse and deceive the American people.

THE SENATE HEARINGS ON GAME SHOW FRAUD WERE FRONT-PAGE NEWS. RIGHT BEFORE STAR WITNESS LOUIS G. COWAN WAS SET TO TESTIFY, HE ENTERED THE HOSPITAL WITH AN ATTACK OF PHLEBITIS.

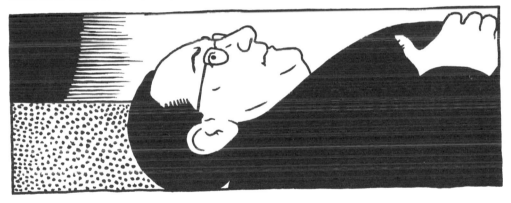

SOON HE WAS FORCED TO RESIGN FROM CBS. HIS CAREER IN MEDIA WAS OVER.

NOW THAT THE DISHONESTY OF THE MEDIA HAD BEEN EXPOSED, EVERY GAME SHOW EVER BECAME SUSPECT. EVEN *QUIZ KIDS*.

IN CLOSED-DOOR TESTIMONY BEFORE THE HOUSE LEGISLATIVE OVERSIGHT COMMITTEE, ONE FORMER PRODUCER OF *QUIZ KIDS* EXPLAINED THAT ALTHOUGH NO QUESTIONS WERE SUPPLIED BEFOREHAND:

AS THE PUBLIC NOW KNEW, SOME SHOWS HAD BEEN "RIGGED," AND SOME HAD BEEN "CONTROLLED." CONTROLLED WAS NOT AS BAD AS RIGGED, BUT THERE WAS A SUGGESTION OF DISHONESTY. WHEN THE PRESS ASKED MY GRANDMOTHER, SHE SAID:

THE PRESS CAUGHT UP WITH MY FATHER, WHO WAS COMPLETING HIS STUDIES AT HARVARD. HIS FATHER HAD JUST DIED.

As far as I'm concerned, the shows were very competitive, although I didn't think they were particularly good.

I know that when I lost, I felt very stupid.

THE FOLLOWING YEAR HE MOVED TO MANSFIELD, CONNECTICUT.

FIVE YEARS LATER, THE HOUSE IN THE WOODS WAS BUILT.

SEVEN YEARS LATER, I WAS BORN.

CHAPTER
8

WHATEVER HAPPENED TO

JOEL KUPPERMAN

If you would be known, and not know, vegetate in a village; if you would know, and not be known, live in a city.

—Charles Caleb Colton, *Lacon*, 1820

THE WORLD GRADUALLY FORGOT ABOUT MY FATHER AND *QUIZ KIDS*.

WHEN I WAS YOUNG, THERE WERE STILL REMINDERS EVERYWHERE.

RICHARD WENT INTO A CAREER IN THE STATE DEPARTMENT. HARVE CHANGED HIS LAST NAME TO BENNETT AND WENT INTO SHOW BUSINESS. HE EVENTUALLY PRODUCED FOUR OF THE *STAR TREK* MOVIES.

RUTHIE BECAME AN EXPERT ON CHILD DEVELOPMENT. IN 1981, SHE SPARKED A RESURGENCE OF PUBLIC INTEREST IN THE SHOW WITH HER BOOK *WHATEVER HAPPENED TO THE QUIZ KIDS?* MY FATHER, OF COURSE, REFUSED TO BE INVOLVED.

A FEW YEARS LATER SHE ARRANGED A CONFERENCE ON THE SHOW.
EX-KIDS WERE INVITED, AS WERE DEVELOPMENTAL EXPERTS AND THE MEDIA.

THE CONFERENCE WAS STAGED AT THE UNIVERSITY OF CONNECTICUT,
WHERE MY FATHER TAUGHT, FOUR MILES FROM OUR HOUSE.

MY FATHER MADE A POINT OF BEING OUT OF THE COUNTRY THAT WEEK. EVERY NEWS STORY ON THE CONFERENCE MENTIONED HIS REFUSAL TO ATTEND.

AFTER THAT, PEOPLE RESUMED FORGETTING.

IT WAS ALL MY FATHER WANTED, TO BE FORGOTTEN AND TO FORGET HIMSELF.

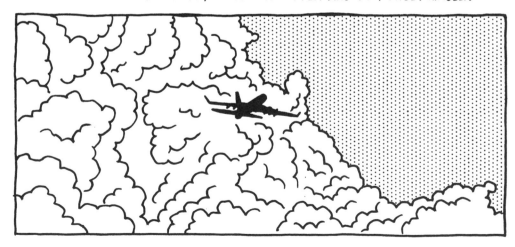

MY MOTHER (A SCANDINAVIAN ARMY BRAT FROM A CONSERVATIVE CHRISTIAN BACKGROUND) AND HE WERE IN SOME WAYS AN UNLIKELY PAIR, BUT THEY SHARED A LOVE OF INTELLECTUAL DISCOVERY AND A DISLIKE OF PHYSICAL INTIMACY.

MOSTLY, THEY ISOLATED THEMSELVES IN THEIR WORK, AND MY SIBLING AND I TRIED TO FIGURE OUT THE WORLD FOR OURSELVES AS BEST WE COULD.

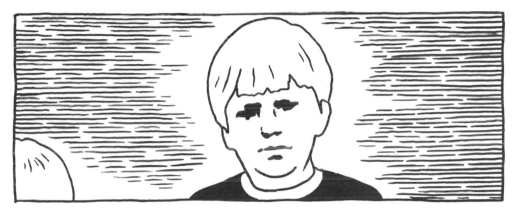

I'M STILL TRYING.

AFTER THAT DAY AT THE GARDEN, MY FATHER STAGED MANY MORE ESCAPES.

HE'D SLIP AWAY WHEN MY MOTHER'S BACK WAS TURNED AND ROAM THE STREETS OF MANHATTAN FOR HOURS BEFORE BEING APPREHENDED.

I SEE THE ESCAPES AS A RETURNING IMPULSE FROM *QUIZ KIDS*. HIS DESIRE TO GET AWAY.

HE HAS A RECURRING PROBLEM WITH DEHYDRATION NOW, AN AVERSION TO
DRINKING WATER.

SURELY A HOLDOVER FROM HIS *QUIZ KIDS* TRAINING. YOU HAD TO BE CAREFUL
ABOUT DRINKING WATER. YOU MIGHT HAVE TO PEE DURING THE SHOW.

EVERYWHERE IN HIS BEHAVIOR, PAST AND PRESENT, I NOW SEE THE MARK OF THE
SHOW. AND, THROUGH HIM, ON ME.

I DON'T KNOW WHAT I THOUGHT THIS BOOK WOULD BE, OR WHAT GOOD IT COULD DO.

THIS DIDN'T HAPPEN.

I STILL THOUGHT I COULD RECOVER HIS SUPPRESSED MEMORIES. I EVEN CONSIDERED HYPNOSIS, ONLY TO FIND THAT RECOVERING MEMORIES THROUGH THAT METHOD HAD BEEN THOROUGHLY DISCREDITED DURING THE 1990s.

NEVERTHELESS, I WAS DETERMINED TO TRY WITH HIM *ONE LAST TIME.*

HE AGREED TO LET ME INTERVIEW HIM AGAIN. HE WAS STILL MOSTLY COGENT, BUT I KNEW THIS WAS PROBABLY THE LAST CHANCE I WOULD HAVE TO HAVE A REAL CONVERSATION WITH MY FATHER. I WADED RIGHT IN.

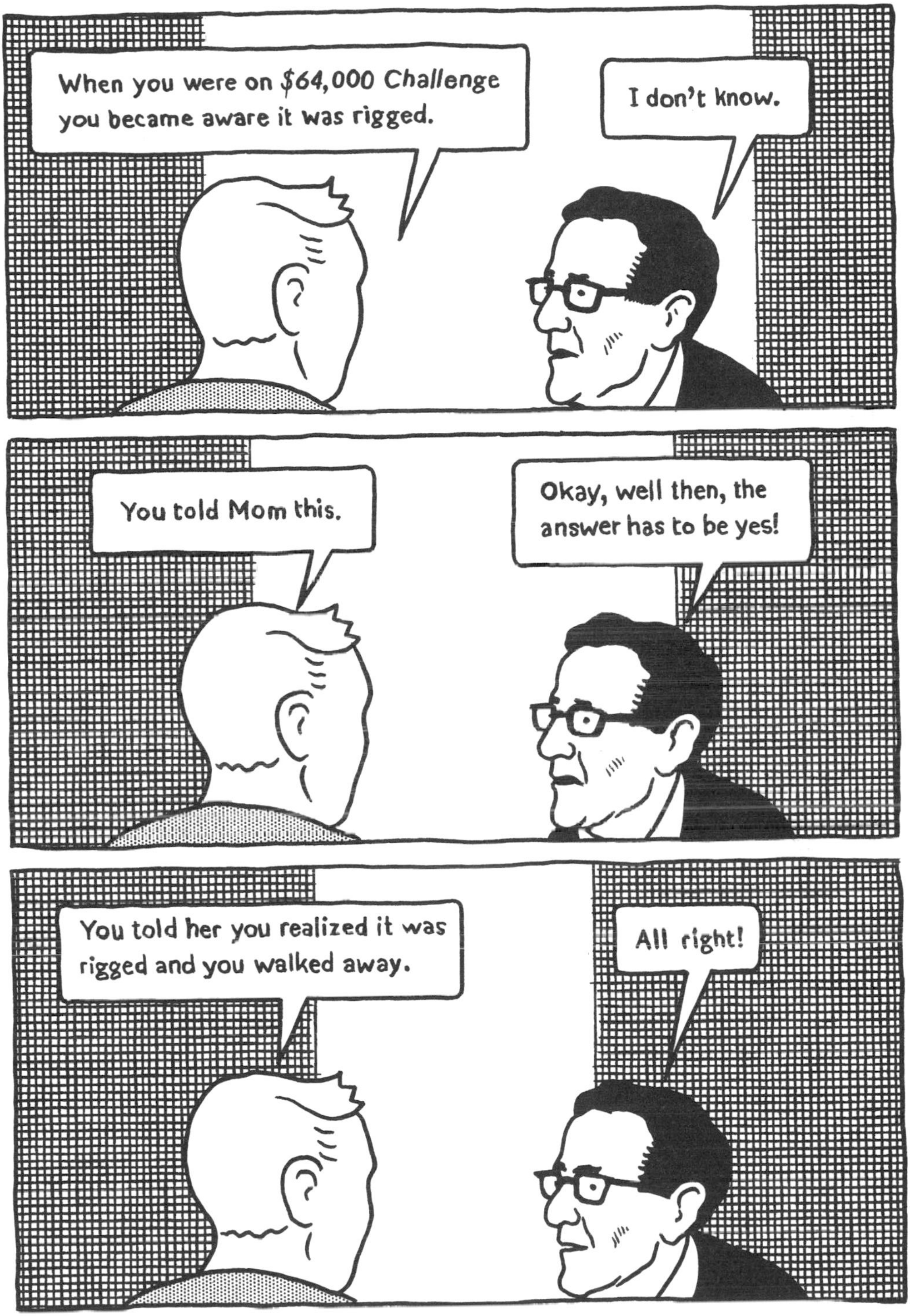
When you were on $64,000 Challenge you became aware it was rigged.
I don't know.
You told Mom this.
Okay, well then, the answer has to be yes!
You told her you realized it was rigged and you walked away.
All right!

I think you suppressed that memory.

I probably did suppress it! Yeah, yeah...

And please don't mention it to anyone.

Of course I'm going to mention it. I'm doing a book!

Okay! I-I don't want...

The quiz show scandal is pretty well documented at this point.

Yeah, but...there could have been a situation in the atmosphere we're talking about in which...

...I was told what a question would be or what would be a question and I have no recollection of that.

BEFORE I STARTED THIS PROJECT, I SAW MY FATHER AS AN ABSENT-MINDED EGGHEAD. NOW I SEE HIM AS A TRAUMA SURVIVOR HIDING BEHIND AN ASSUMED PERSONA DESIGNED TO DEFLECT HOSTILITY.

A FRIEND OF MY PARENTS TOLD ME HOW, DURING HIS FIRST YEARS IN MANSFIELD, HE'D BECOME ILL AND HAVE TO LEAVE THE ROOM IF SOMEONE HE DIDN'T KNOW BROUGHT UP THE SHOW OR EVEN MENTIONED TELEVISION.

ALL THROUGH MY CHILDHOOD, ANY MENTION OF THE SHOW WOULD MAKE HIM TENSE AND WITHDRAWN.

I think you would've been extremely angry at Grandma.

Oh I was, definitely, yes.

HIS BULLYING UNIVERSITY OF CHICAGO ROOMMATE CLAIMED HE WOKE UP EVERY NIGHT SCREAMING.

You were angry?

Well, angry is too strong a word.

She was in some ways a very nice person, but she also created situations which she should've known were bad for me.

She pressured you to stay on *Quiz Kids*—

Definitely. I can remember feeling I've got to get away from this, and it just wasn't possible. I was very clear about the fact that a lot of people depended on me doing my best.

I felt I was trapped, even when there was nothing peculiar or dishonest. I felt that I was trapped in a role that would make the kind of people I would really like to know... not interested in spending time with me.

I KNOW THE FEELING.

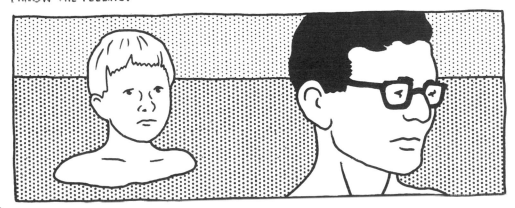

AT MY FAMILY'S CORE WAS A BLANKNESS, A LACK OF GENUINE CONNECTION OR THE SHARED WILL TO PRETEND.

EXCHANGES WERE CHARACTERIZED BY A FORCED LIGHTNESS COVERING A REFUSAL TO VERBALIZE ANYTHING THAT MIGHT CAUSE DISCOMFORT OR PAIN.

THAT BEGAN WITH NOT BRINGING UP THE SHOW. EVER.

WHEN YOU AVOID TALKING ABOUT ONE CONSPICUOUS THING IN A FAMILY, SOON YOU STOP TALKING ABOUT ANY CONSPICUOUS THINGS IN THE FAMILY. IT'S LIKE A FORM OF ROT.

MY FATHER'S EARLY STARDOM BECAME A PIECE OF TRIVIA. AN ODD FACT THAT DIDN'T REALLY MEAN ANYTHING, EVEN AS IT INFLUENCED EVERY ASPECT OF OUR LIVES.

LIVING IN THIS HOUSE DESIGNED TO LOOK OLD, SURROUNDED BY OLD ART AND OLD BOOKS, MY FATHER WENT INSIDE HIMSELF. IN MANY WAYS, HE SAID "NO" TO THE FUTURE.

MANSFIELD WAS A STIFLING PLACE TO GROW UP. PEOPLE ARE INWARD, ANTISOCIAL. THEY DON'T LIKE KIDS. THERE'S NOTHING TO DO AND NOWHERE TO GO.

HE FELT SAFER HIDING OUT THERE, BUT IT MADE THE REST OF US MISERABLE.

STUCK TOGETHER IN THAT CRAMPED HOUSE, WE SHOUTED AND YELLED AND SCREAMED AT EACH OTHER.

1970.

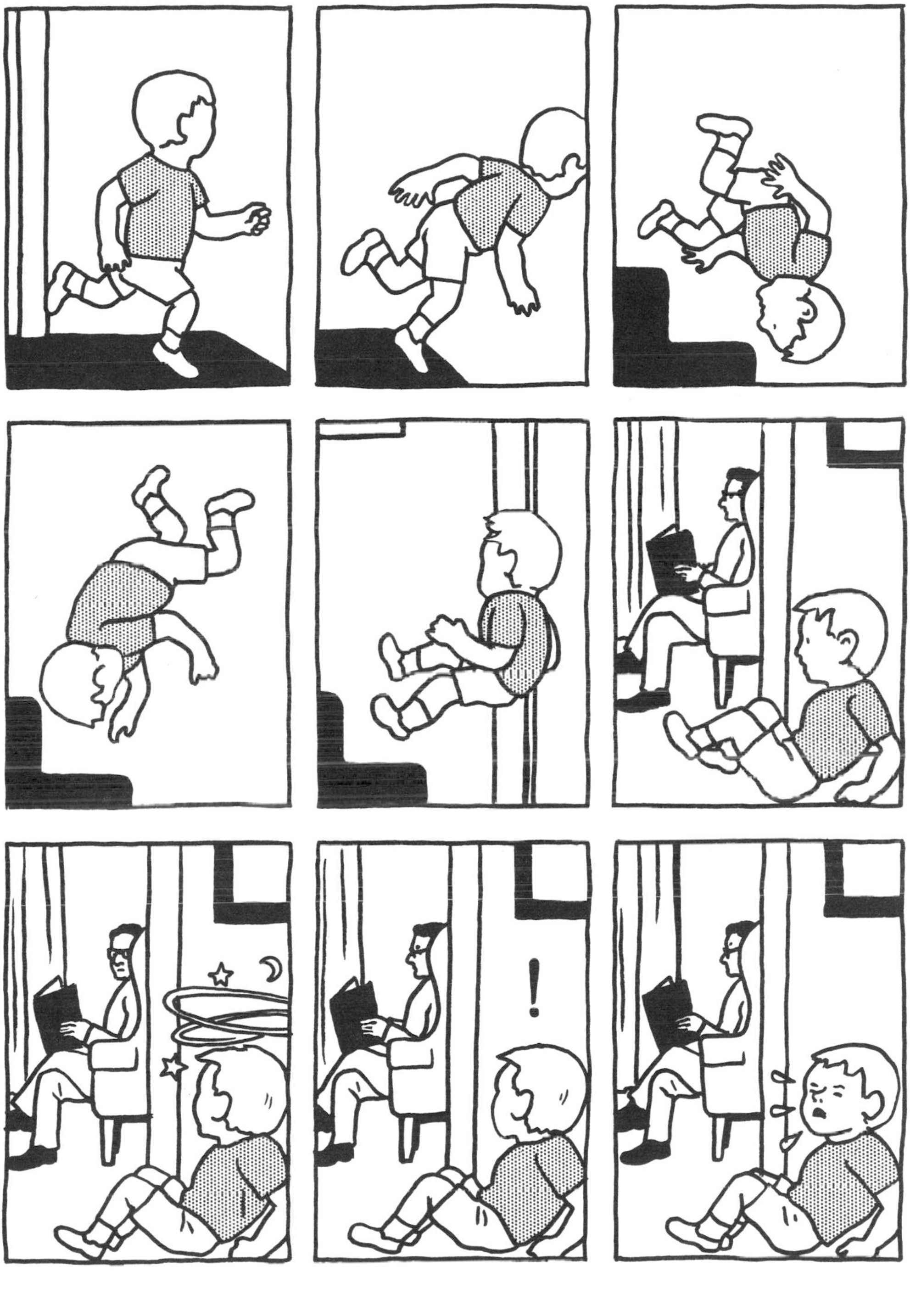
!

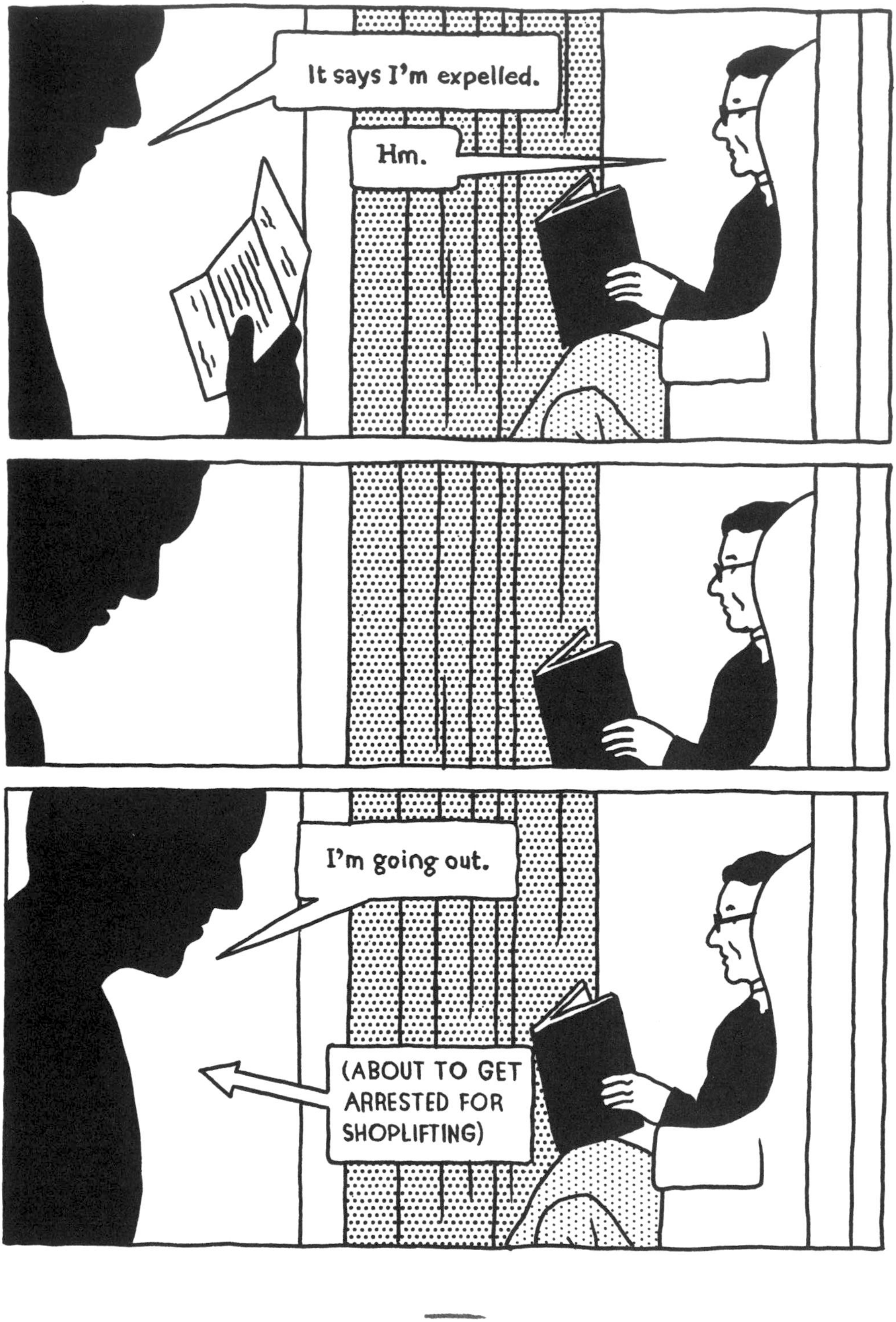
It says I'm expelled.
Hm.
I'm going out.
(ABOUT TO GET ARRESTED FOR SHOPLIFTING)

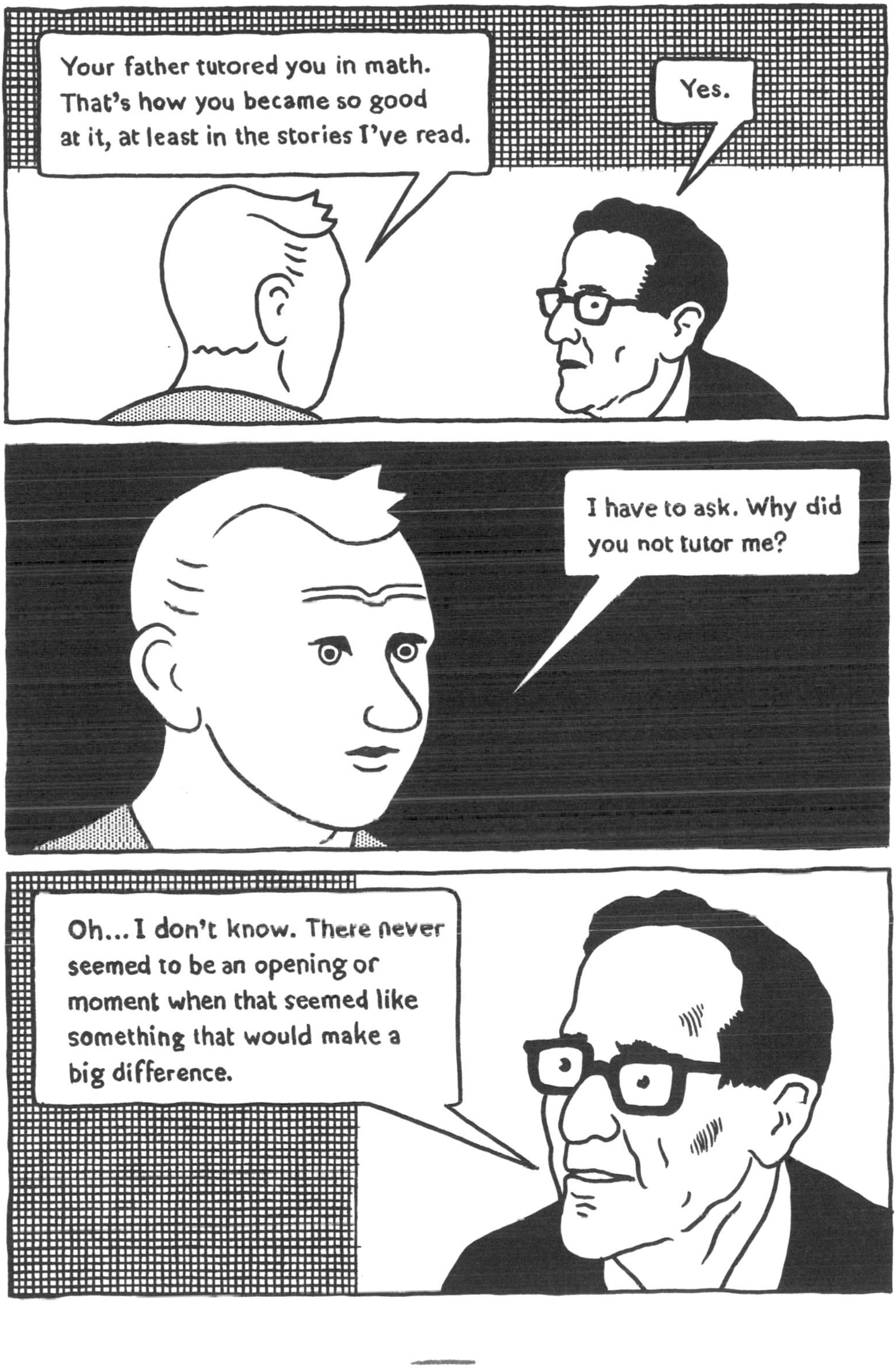
Your father tutored you in math. That's how you became so good at it, at least in the stories I've read.
Yes.
I have to ask. Why did you not tutor me?
Oh... I don't know. There never seemed to be an opening or moment when that seemed like something that would make a big difference.

I should have thought about you more, because... I think my assumption was simply that you were a bright kid, you would do well in school, and that you would find your own way out...

I mean, it didn't occur to me that I should take a hand in steering you... Basically it never occurred to me that I should have a particular obligation to develop your opportunities and understanding...

Especially since, during the period we're talking about, I was out of the picture a lot of the time. I would've had to go back and construct a relationship, and nobody suggested I do that...

Construct a relationship?

With you.

No one suggested you should do that.

No one at all. It just didn't occur to me. I'm sorry, I should have, but I had a lot on my shoulders. I'm sorry, but you're making me feel almost guilty, that I should have been spending time with you.

Well, I think guilt is a waste of time but I kind of think you should've. Yeah.

Usually in the kind of situation we're discussing, someone says, "Why don't you" and no one said that. So I could've done it, but it just never occurred to me, and I... I'm feeling more and more sorry about it.

I really feel if I'd been more alert, I would've spent more time with you.

I WISH WE'D HAD THIS CONVERSATION YEARS AGO.

It's like when that professor told you to go to England. It really hadn't occurred to you?

Yeah. It hadn't occurred to me...

You were the smartest kid in the world, good at answering questions, but in your life you needed someone to tell you what to do.

I was still a kid, and I had no clear clues as to what I wanted to do.

The people that I would end up talking about this stuff with were extremely hostile. They really were very hostile!

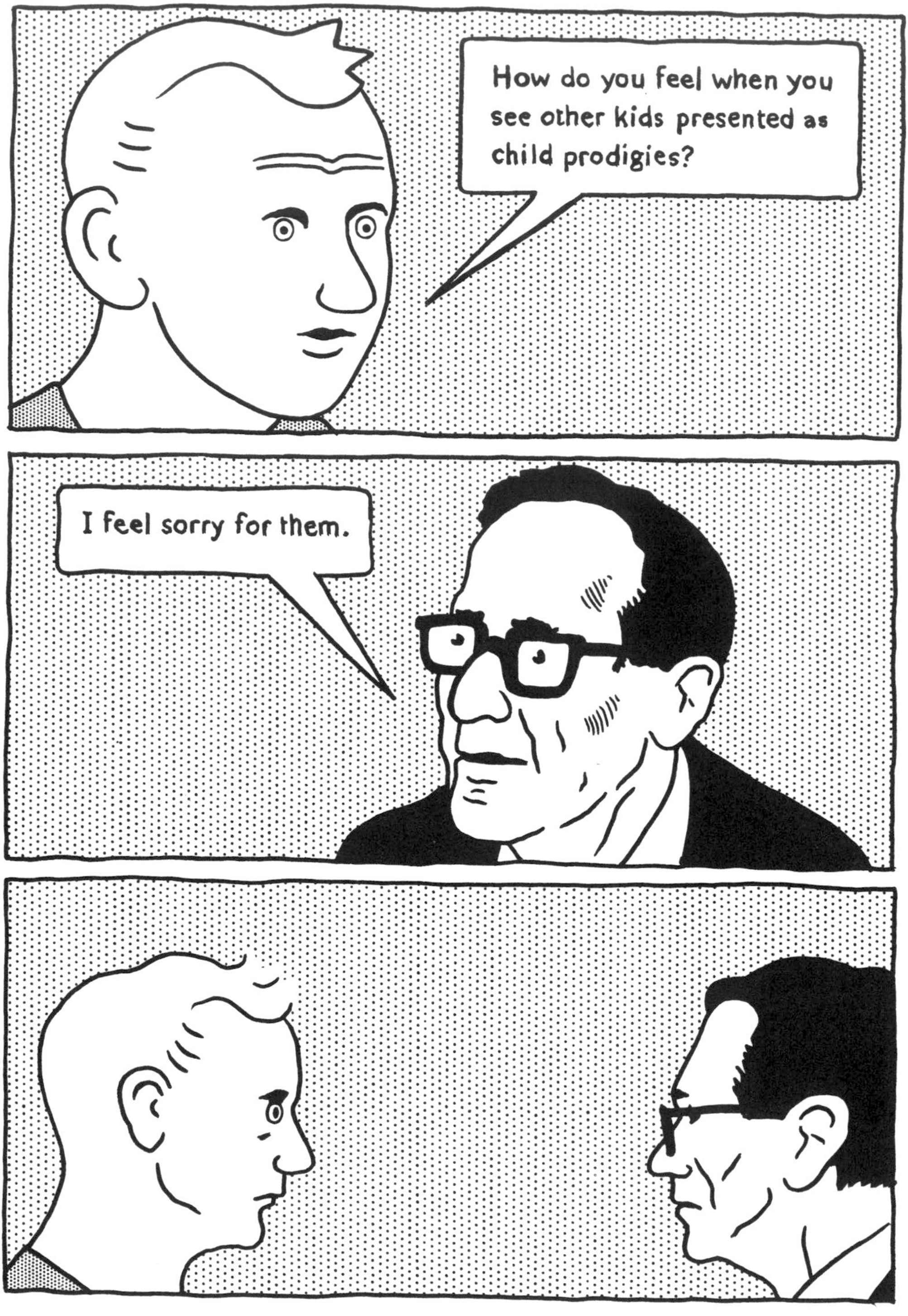
How do you feel when you see other kids presented as child prodigies?
I feel sorry for them.

I THINK I'VE LEARNED ENOUGH.

I'VE GOTTEN ALL THE ANSWERS I'M GOING TO GET FROM MY FATHER.

BUT THAT'S OKAY. BECAUSE I KNOW THIS: THE REAL ANSWERS DON'T COME FROM OTHER PEOPLE. THEY **CAN'T** TELL YOU WHAT TO **DO.**

THE REAL ANSWERS COME FROM WITHIN.

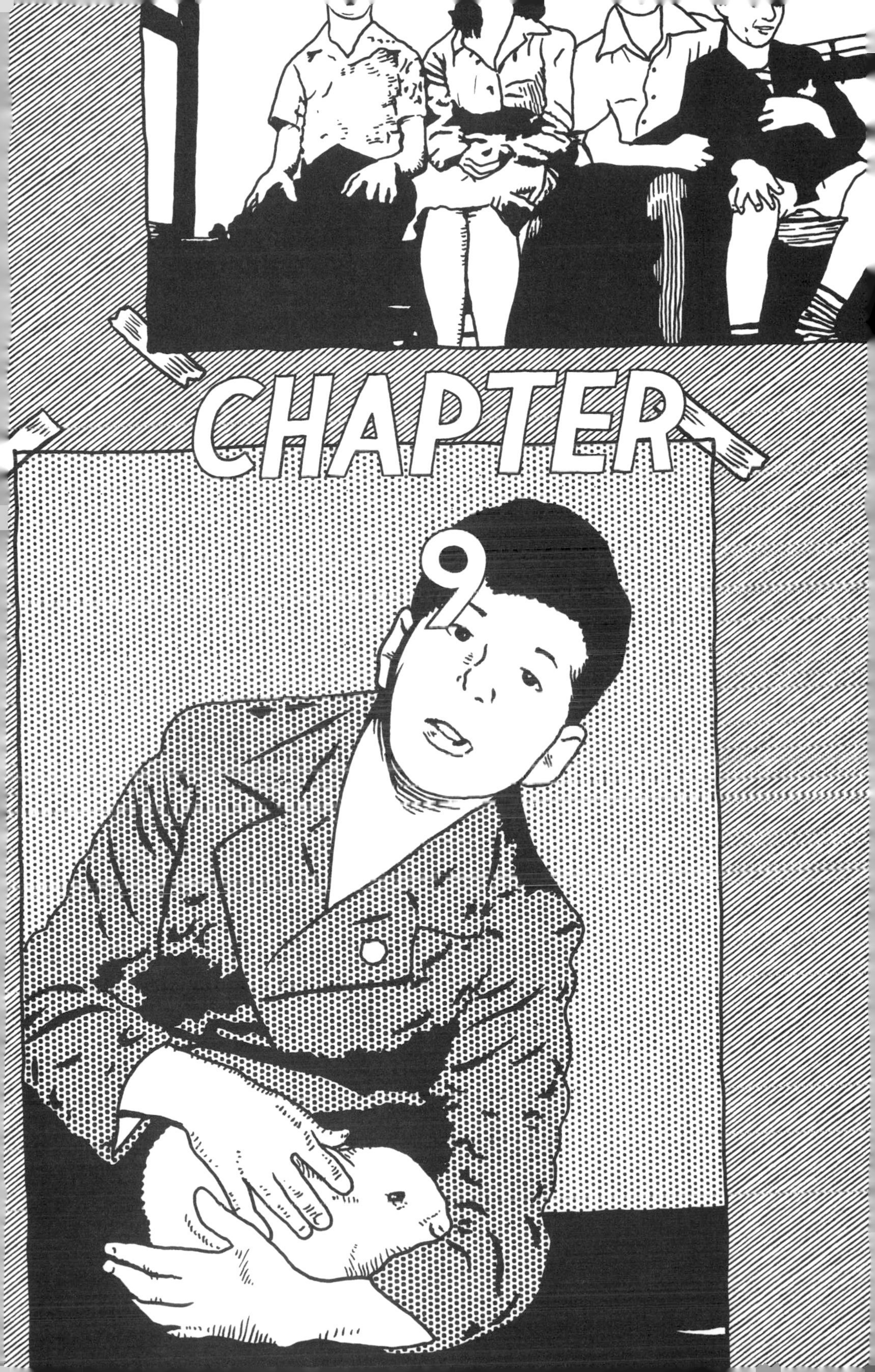
CHAPTER
9

'I have answered three questions, and that is enough,'
Said his father; 'don't give yourself airs!
Do you think I can listen all day to such stuff?
Be off, or I'll kick you downstairs!'

—Lewis Carroll,

Alice's Adventures in Wonderland

RRYMORE

at the age of
after her stage
liss Barrymore
ooliath blies

MY FATHER WON'T BE ABLE TO READ THIS BOOK.

IT'S BEEN A COUPLE OF YEARS, AND THE DEMENTIA HAS STRIPPED AWAY HIS ABILITY TO UNDERSTAND PRACTICALLY ANYTHING.

HIS GRANDSON AND I VISIT HIM IN HIS NEW HOME. HE'S GENERALLY SERENE.

BUT IF I MENTION THE SHOW OR THIS BOOK, A PROFOUNDLY TROUBLED LOOK MOVES ACROSS HIS FACE.

HE DOESN'T EVEN KNOW WHY ANYMORE.

AUNT HARRIET IS STILL VERY MENTALLY PRESENT.

...he felt guilty? He shouldn't have... it was our parents' fault...

I TELL MY SON "I DON'T WANT YOU TO BE A SUCCESSFUL CHILD. I WANT YOU TO BE A SUCCESSFUL ADULT."

BOYS MODEL THEMSELVES ON THEIR FATHERS. HE'S ALREADY A DIFFICULT ARTIST.

I UNDERSTAND IT ALL NOW. DAD COULDN'T SHARE WITH ME ANYTHING FROM BEING A QUIZ KID. BECAUSE HE'D REJECTED EVERY BIT OF IT. HE'D DONE IT TO SURVIVE.

ALL HE COULD TEACH ME WAS WHAT HE'D LEARNED AFTERWARD: KEEP YOUR HEAD DOWN. DON'T ATTRACT ATTENTION. KEEP QUIET. BLEND IN.

THE LESSONS OF A TRAUMATIZED EX-CHILD STAR.

AND IT'S SAD HE DIDN'T ENJOY IT ALL MORE. BEYOND ALL THE FAMOUS PEOPLE, BEYOND ALL THE HISTORY HE SAW OR WAS PART OF, BEYOND ALL HIS EXPERIENCES, WAS AN ESSENTIAL TRUTH:

HE REALLY MEANT SOMETHING TO A LOT OF PEOPLE. MANY PEOPLE HATED HIM, BUT MANY PEOPLE LOVED HIM TOO.

Mrs. Virgil Johnson of Tulsa, Oklahoma, reports that the Washington Monument is sinking 1/40 of an inch a year.

Let us consider it is 555 feet high. If it continues to sink at the rate of 1/40th of an inch a year, how long will it be before it disappears from sight?

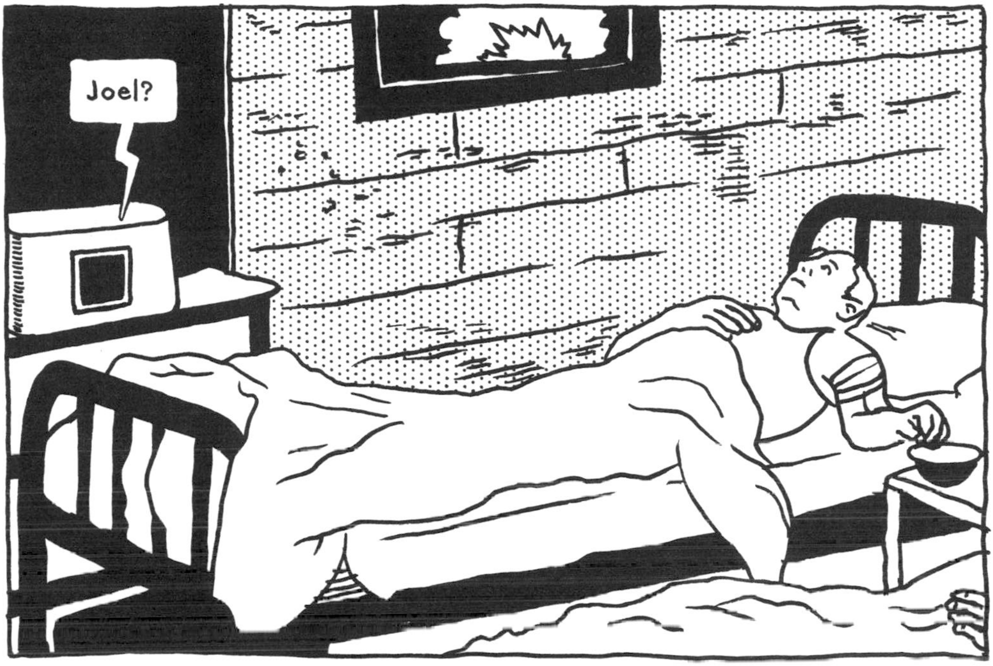
Joel?

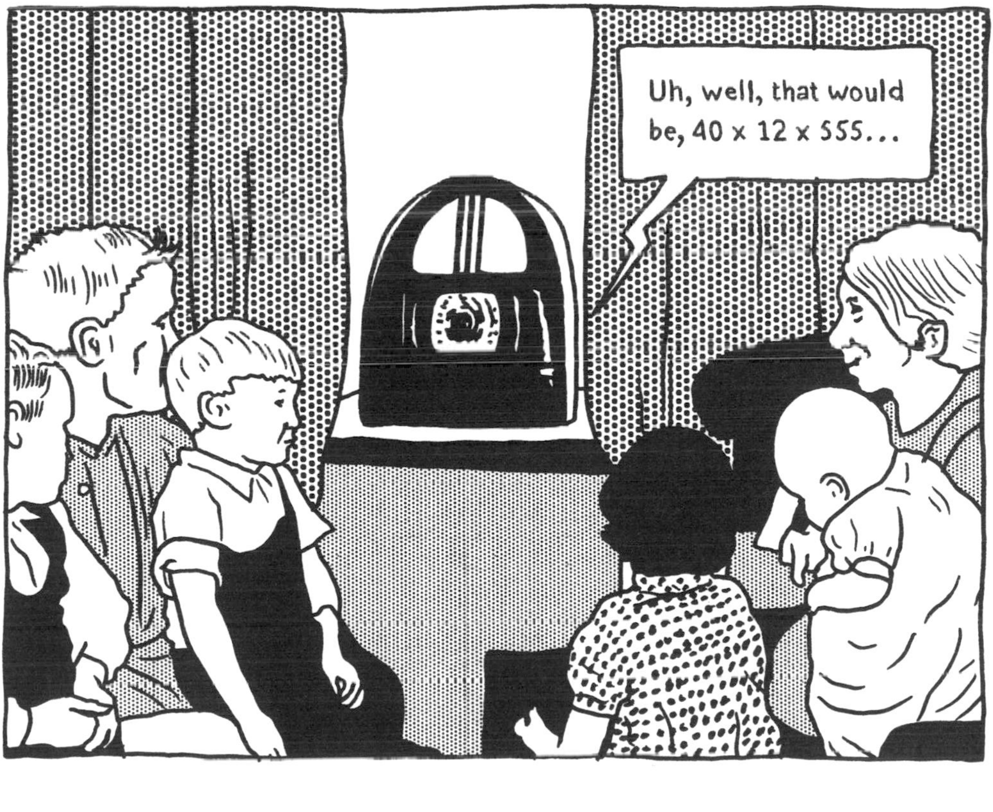
Uh, well, that would be, 40 x 12 x 555...

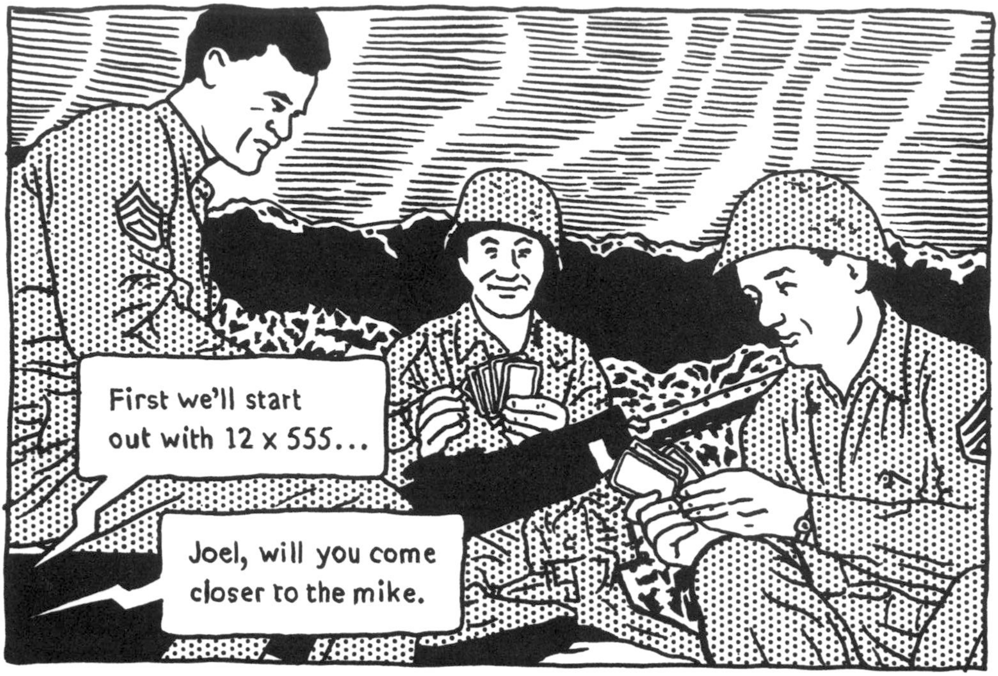
First we'll start out with 12 x 555...
Joel, will you come closer to the mike.

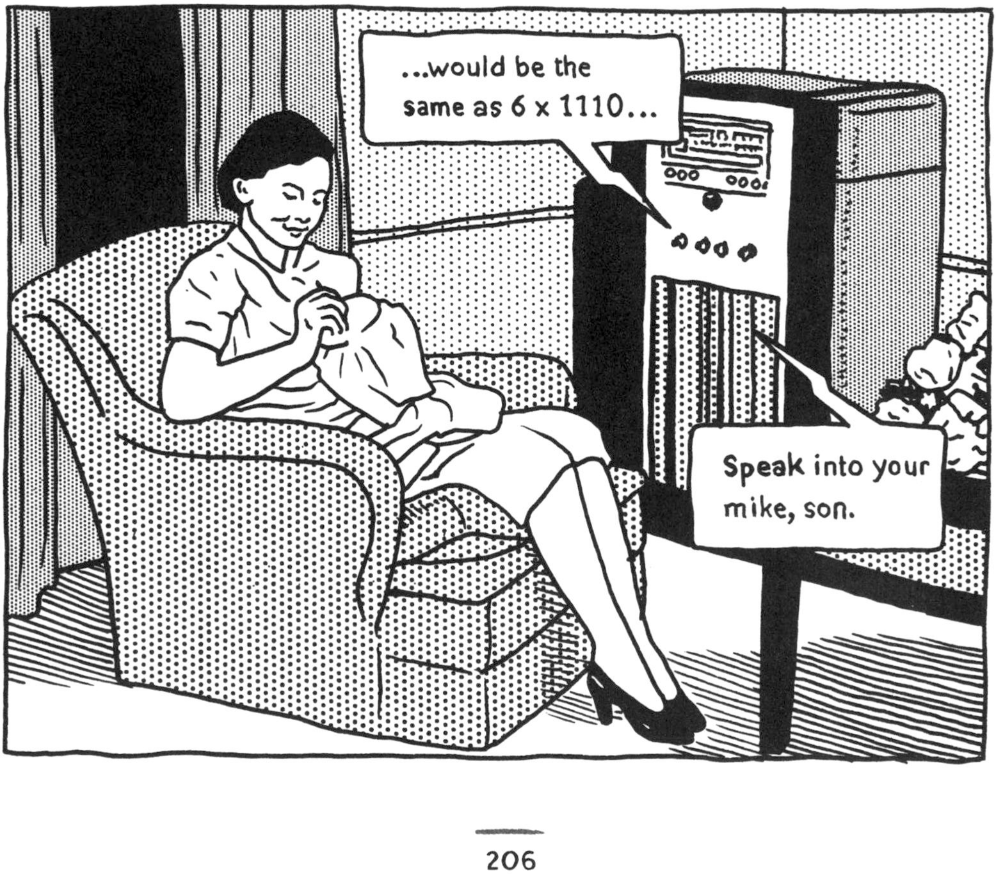
...would be the same as 6 x 1110...
Speak into your mike, son.

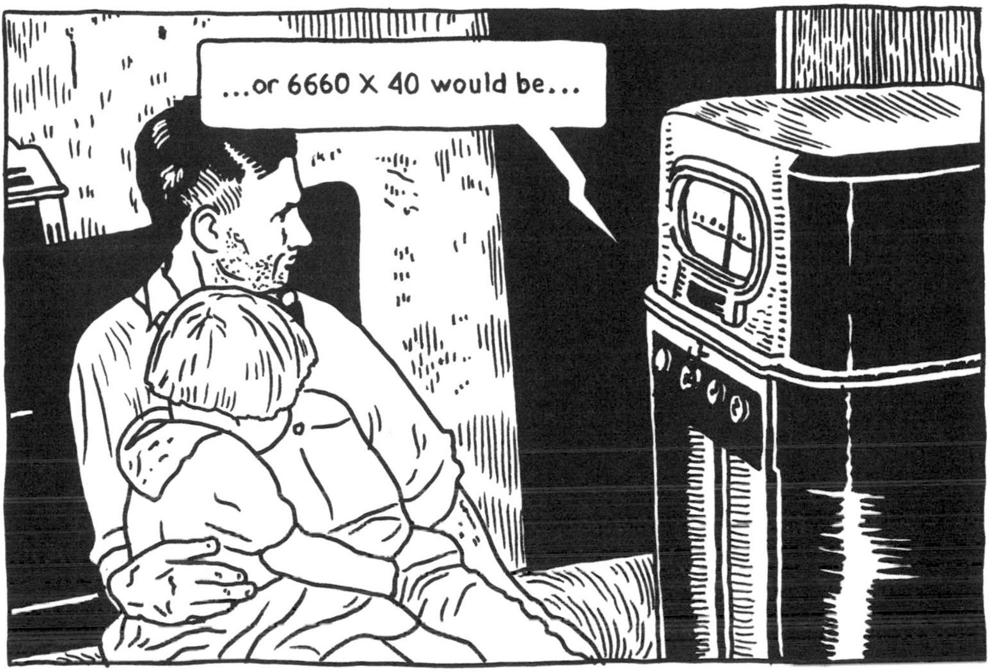
...or 6660 X 40 would be...

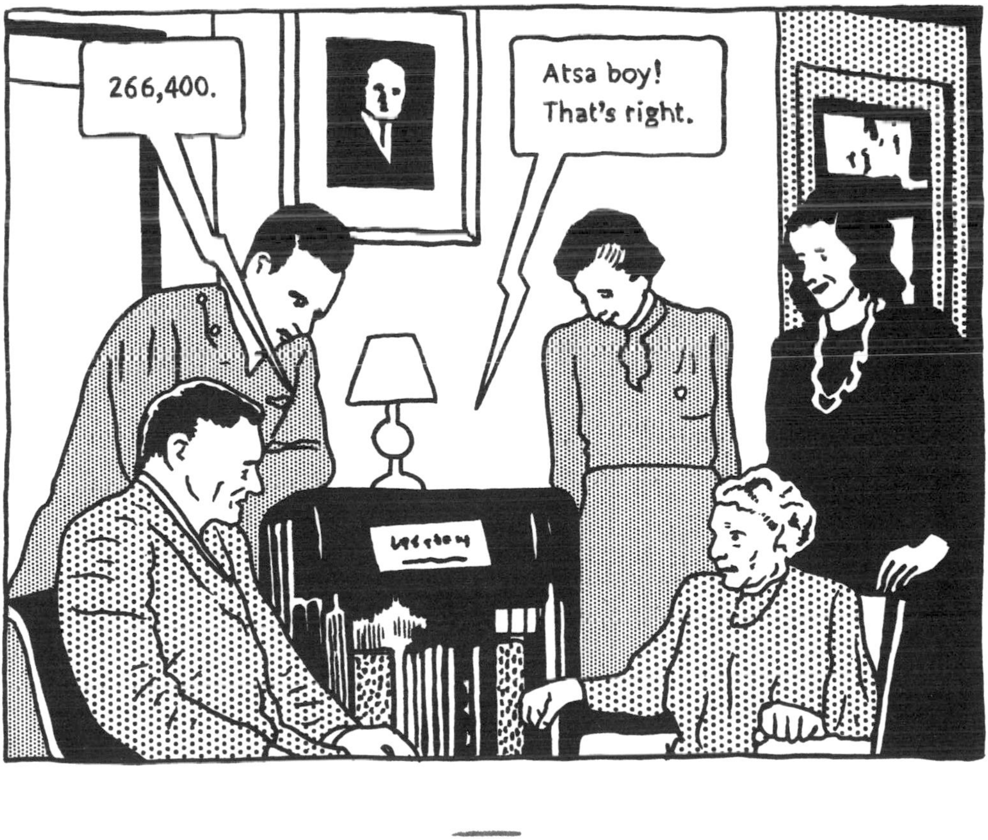
266,400.
Atsa boy! That's right.

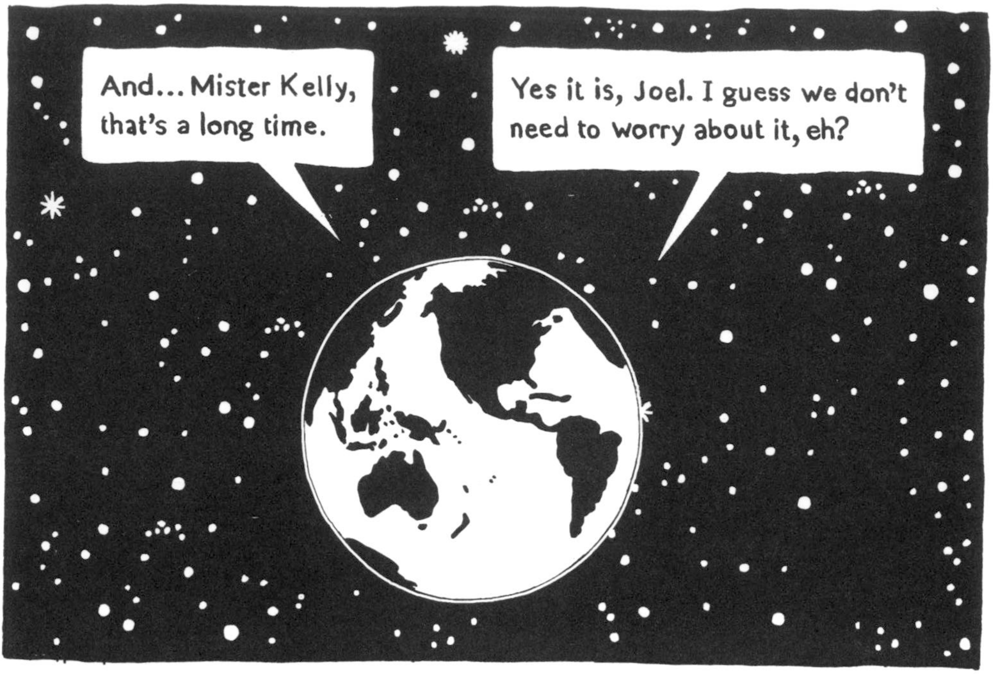
And... Mister Kelly, that's a long time.
Yes it is, Joel. I guess we don't need to worry about it, eh?

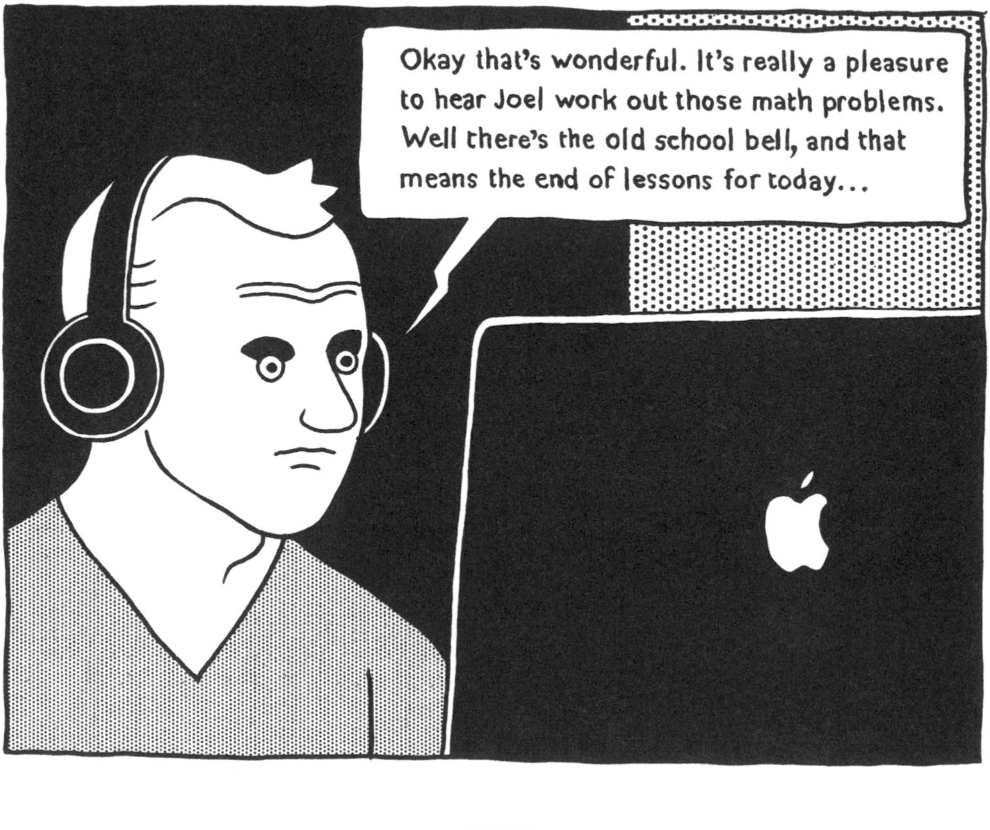
Okay that's wonderful. It's really a pleasure to hear Joel work out those math problems. Well there's the old school bell, and that means the end of lessons for today...

HE WAS PART OF HISTORY. THEN FOR A LONG TIME HE HATED IT AND WANTED TO FORGET. THEN BRIEFLY HE DIDN'T CARE. THEN HE FORGOT FOR GOOD.

THE STORY OF JOEL KUPPERMAN, QUIZ KID.

IT HAPPENED IN THE PAST, WHERE EVERY LITTLE THING WAS DIFFERENT AND PEOPLE HAD MYSTERIOUS AND SOMETIMES SELF-DEFEATING MOTIVES.

STARING AT HISTORY IS LIKE STARING AT ANY ABSTRACT PATTERN. YOU START TO SEE THINGS.

MY FATHER HAD A LONG AND DISTINGUISHED CAREER AS A PHILOSOPHY PROFESSOR. HE WROTE, HE TRAVELED. HE INFLUENCED THOUSANDS OF YOUNG MINDS.

HE DID ESCAPE *QUIZ KIDS*.

NOW HERE I COME DRAGGING IT ALL OUT AGAIN.

SO HERE'S THE $64,000 QUESTION:

DOES THIS MAKE ME A GOOD SON, OR A BAD ONE?

I THINK I HAD TO DO THIS. IT'S NOT GOOD TO LIVE IN THE PAST, BUT IT'S NOT GOOD TO IGNORE IT EITHER.

FOR MYSELF AND MY FAMILY. AND FOR HIM TOO. THE STORY NEEDED TO BE TOLD.

DIDN'T IT?

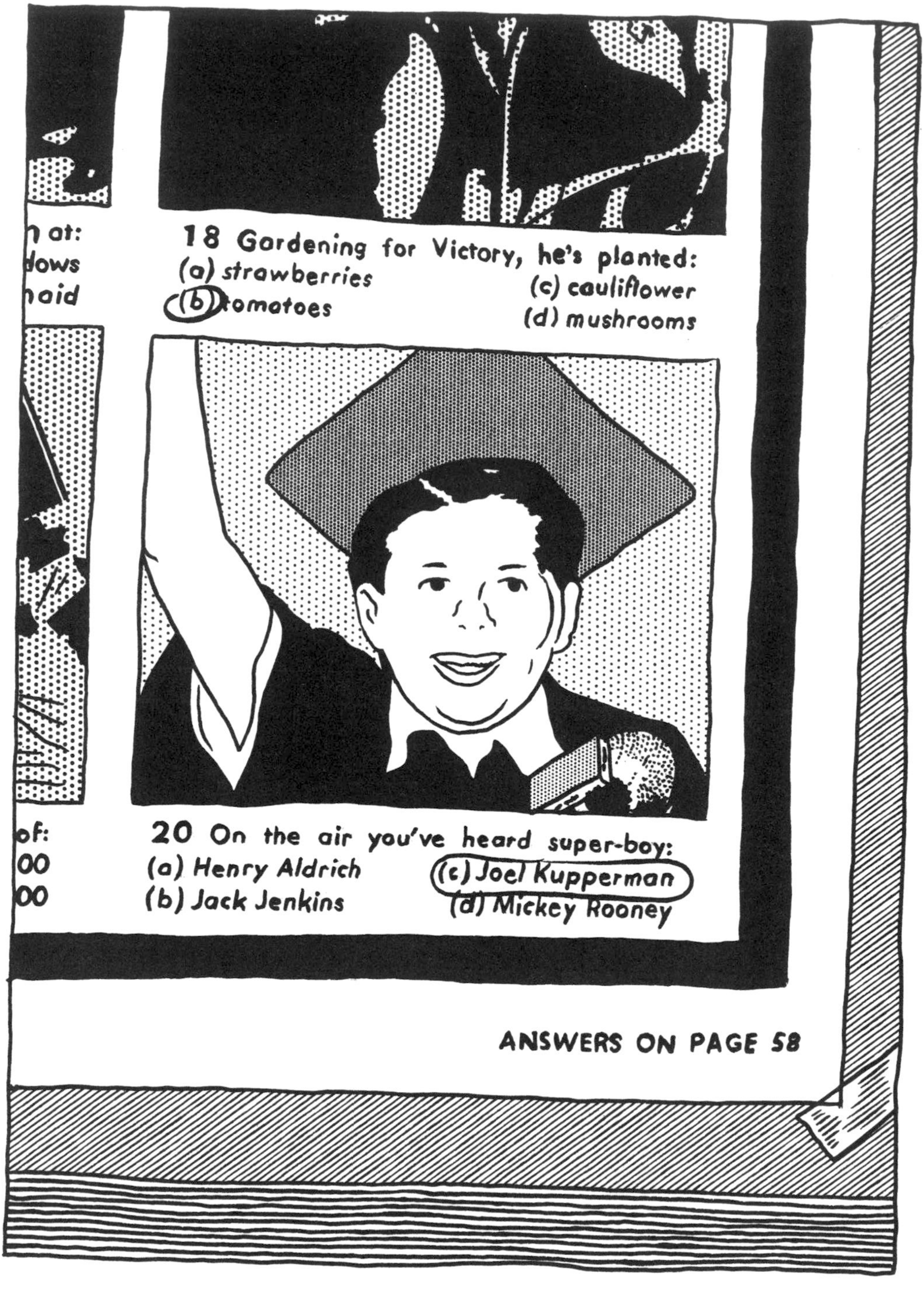
n at:
dows
naid
18 Gardening for Victory, he's planted:
(a) strawberries
(b) tomatoes
(c) cauliflower
(d) mushrooms
of:
00
00
20 On the air you've heard super-boy:
(a) Henry Aldrich
(b) Jack Jenkins
(c) Joel Kupperman
(d) Mickey Rooney
ANSWERS ON PAGE 58

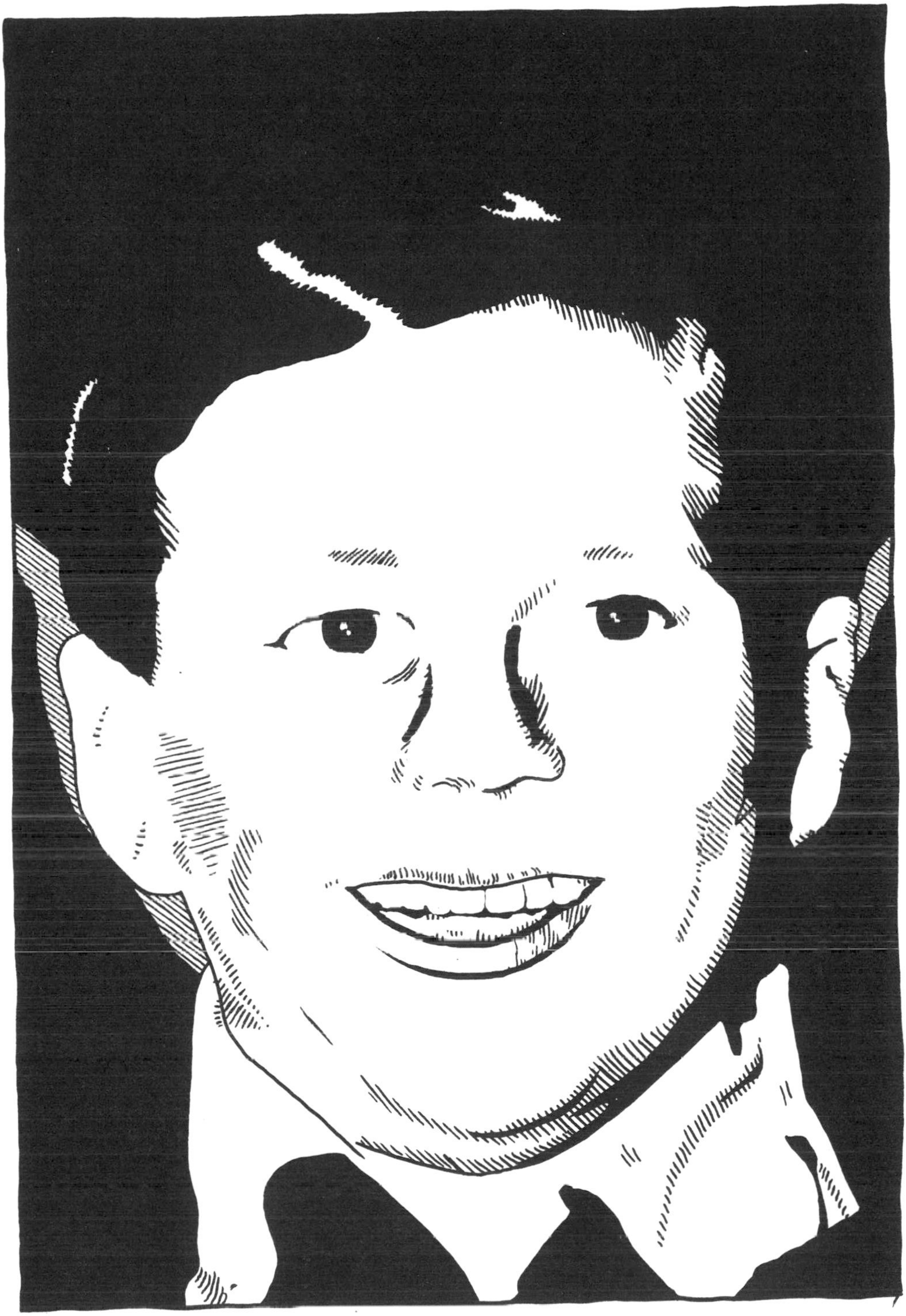

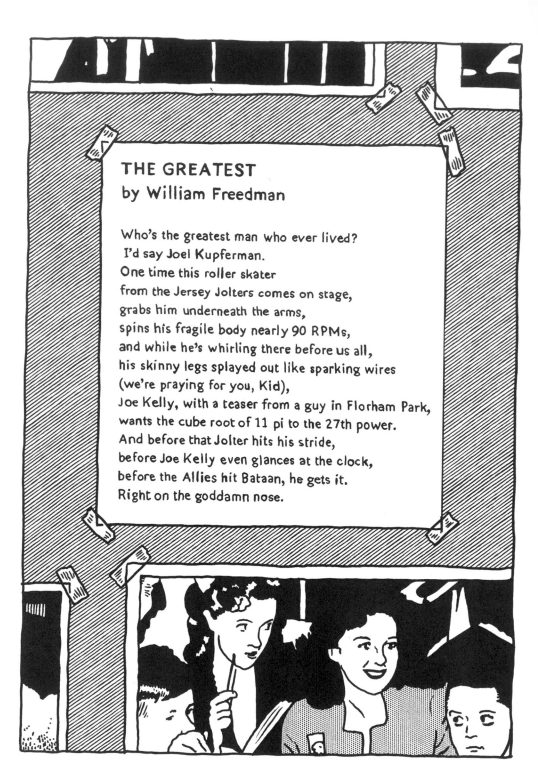

THE GREATEST
by William Freedman

Who's the greatest man who ever lived?
 I'd say Joel Kupferman.
One time this roller skater
from the Jersey Jolters comes on stage,
grabs him underneath the arms,
spins his fragile body nearly 90 RPMs,
and while he's whirling there before us all,
his skinny legs splayed out like sparking wires
(we're praying for you, Kid),
Joe Kelly, with a teaser from a guy in Florham Park,
wants the cube root of 11 pi to the 27th power.
And before that Jolter hits his stride,
before Joe Kelly even glances at the clock,
before the Allies hit Bataan, he gets it.
Right on the goddamn nose.

I'm in Israel now,
Row 21, Seat 7, Section K
in the Roman amphitheater in Caesaria
where Rabbi Akiva,
Heaven bless his memory and soothe his skin,
96 wrinkled butter-fleshed years,
was flayed alive
(the 7th layer brought the plebies to their feet)
for answering questions he shouldn't have asked.
96 but he could take it.
Even the flayer gave him a hand.
Now Barenboim's up there with Ludwig's 9th
(you know the place: where the tympani
and cellos fight it out),
and a great white gull
shot from the window of the hidden sea
just soared above the shell,
pounded wings to match those drums,
spread out like cellos at full bow
and just kept going.
Akiva, you were great out there,
and Danny, Ludwig, Nature too,
don't think I don't appreciate you all.
But oh my God, Joel Kupferman,
I miss you so.

OCTOBER NO. 79 10¢

TRUE

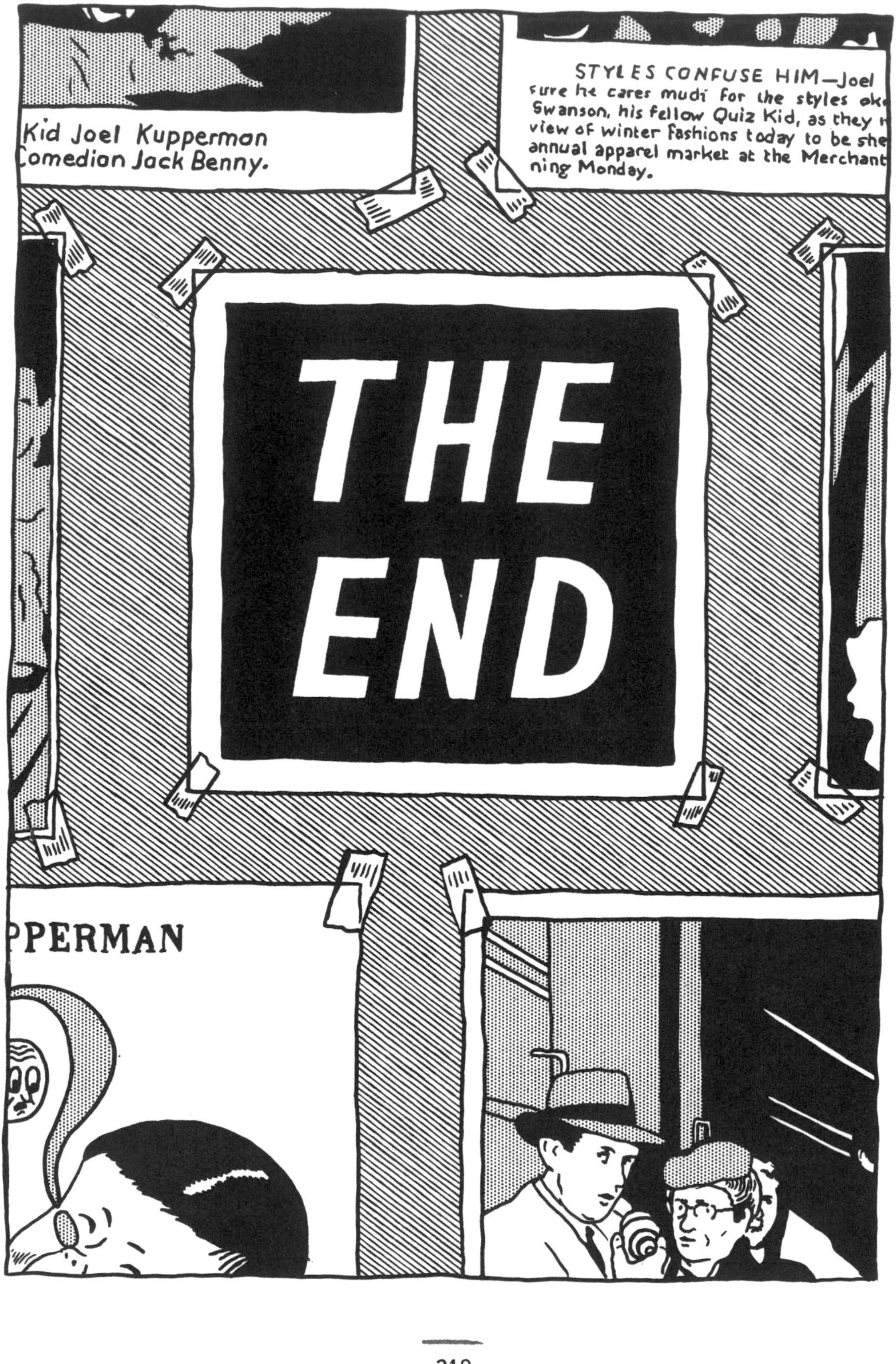
Kid Joel Kupperman
Comedian Jack Benny.
STYLES CONFUSE HIM—Joel
sure he cares much for the styles
Swanson, his fellow Quiz Kid, as they
view of winter fashions today to be she
annual apparel market at the Merchant
ning Monday.
THE END
PPERMAN

THANK YOU TO

My editor, Adam Wilson, for his enthusiasm and encouragement;
my agent, Scott Mendel, for his wisdom and guidance;
Jane Klain at the Paley Center Library, who was invaluably helpful;
my friend Julie Klausner, who was supportive and thoughtful;
my son, Ulysses Kupperman Dougherty, who inspires me every day.
And my wife, Muire Dougherty, who motivated me, pushed me,
made it all possible and put up with so much.

Also thanks to:

Harriet Moss · Arthur Smith · Marianne Ways · Janet Robertson
Neil Martinson · Nina Jordan · Danny Hellman · Robert Popper
Stanley Freedman

and my parents, Karen Ordahl Kupperman and Joel Kupperman.

A PARTIAL LIST OF SOURCES

Anderson, Kent. *Television Fraud: The History and Implications of The Quiz Show Scandals.* Westport, CT: Greenwood Press, 1978.

Feldman, Ruth Duskin. *Whatever Happened to The Quiz Kids? Perils and Profits of Growing Up Gifted.* Chicago: Chicago Review Press, 1982.

Freedman, William. "The Greatest." The *Antioch Review,* Vol. 43, No. 4 (Autumn 1985).

Gardner, Martin A. *Quiz Kids: The Radio Program with the Smartest Children in America, 1940–1953.* Jefferson, NC: McFarland & Company, Inc., 2013.

Hickok, Eliza Merill. *The Quiz Kids.*
Boston: Houghton Mifflin Company, 1947.

Nachman, Gerald. *Raised on Radio.* New York: Pantheon Books, 1998.

Ritchie, Michael. *Please Stand By: A Prehistory of Television.*
New York: The Overlook Press, 1994.

Roth, Philip. *The Anatomy Lesson.* New York:
Farrar, Straus and Giroux, 1983.

Salinger, J. D. *Raise High the Roof Beam, Carpenters and Seymour: An Introduction.* Boston: Little, Brown and Company, 1963.

Skolsky, Sidney. "Hollywords." September 9, 1943.

Terkel, Studs. *Working: People Talk About What They Do All Day and How They Feel About What They Do.* New York: Pantheon, 1974.

Wilson, Earl. *I Am Gazing into My 8-Ball.*
Garden City, New York: The Sun Dial Press, 1945.